OSPREY AIRCRAFT OF THE ACES • 108

P-38 Lightning Aces of the 82nd Fighter Group

SERIES EDITOR: TONY HOLMES

OSPREY AIRCRAFT OF THE ACES • 108

P-38 Lightning Aces of the 82nd Fighter Group

Steve Blake

OSPREY
PUBLISHING

Front Cover
On 11 May 1943, Lt Col John W Weltman, CO of the 82nd Fighter Group (FG), led 54 P-38s of its 95th and 96th Fighter Squadrons (FS) off from their base at Berteaux, in Algeria, for a then-typical medium bomber escort mission. They shepherded B-25s of the 310th Bomb Group (BG) and B-26s of the 17th and 320th BGs to the harbour at Marsala, on the western tip of Sicily. After the bombing, which did a great deal of damage to both the harbour facilities and the town itself, the USAAF aircraft withdrew a few miles to the west over the Mediterranean in order to re-group for the trip home.

At that point enemy fighters – four Bf 109s, four Italian Macchi C.200s and a lone Fw 190 – attacked the American formation. Two of the Bf 109s from II./JG 27, then based at nearby Trapani, made an ill-advised head-on attack on a P-38 flight led by the 95th FS CO, Capt Ernest K 'Hawk' Osher, evidently disregarding the Lightning's potent nose-mounted armament of four 0.50-cal machine guns and a single 20 mm cannon. Osher was credited with destroying one of them, whilst 2Lt John L Dean damaged the other and 1Lt Samuel A 'Sammy' Hawes of the 96th FS damaged the Fw 190. No Lightnings were lost, although one of the B-26s crash-landed on the way home.

This was the last aerial claim made by Capt Osher, who had assumed command of the 95th just ten days earlier, giving him a total of five destroyed and two damaged, and making him the 82nd FG's eighth ace. Osher served as squadron CO until the end of July, by which time he had been promoted to major.

Osher was at the controls of P-38F-15 43-2112 on 11 May, this aircraft being his personally assigned Lightning. It displayed the unit code letters 'AS' on its outer coolant radiator housings and the name *"THE SAD SACK"* (after the popular cartoon character) on its nose. The Bf 109 claimed by the fighter that day was this extraordinary aircraft's 11th confirmed kill. 43-2112's career with the 95th FS lasted a lot longer than 'Hawk' Osher's, *"THE SAD SACK"* finally meeting its end when the fighter was scrapped after being badly damaged by flak over Yugoslavia on 29 May 1944. By then the aeroplane had flown an amazing 183 combat missions, and been credited with 16 aerial victories (*Cover artwork by Mark Postlethwaite*)

First published in Great Britain in 2012 by Osprey Publishing
Midland House, West Way, Botley, Oxford, OX2 0PH
44-02 23rd Street, Suite 219, Long Island City, NY, 11101, USA

E-mail; info@ospreypublishing.com

Osprey Publishing is part of the Osprey Group

A CIP catalogue record for this book is available from the British Library

ISBN: 978 1 84908 743 8
PDF e-book ISBN: 978 1 84908 744 5
e-Pub ISBN: 978 1 78096 871 1

Edited by Tony Holmes
Page design by Tony Truscott
Cover Artwork by Mark Postlethwaite
Aircraft Profiles by Chris Davey
Index by Alan Thatcher
Originated by PDQ Digital Media Solutions
Printed and bound in China through Bookbuilders

12 13 14 15 16 17   10 9 8 7 6 5 4 3 2 1

Osprey Publishing is supporting the Woodland Trust, the UK's leading woodland conservation charity, by funding the dedication of trees.

www.ospreypublishing.com

ACKNOWLEDGEMENTS
I would like to thank the dozens of 82nd FG veterans and their family members – too many to mention all of them here by name – who have provided me and my old colleague John Stanaway with so much material over the past 30 years, including copies of photographs, official documents, contemporary letters and diaries and newspaper and magazine articles. And particularly, in the case of the veteran pilots, for their detailed and intimate recollections of fighting the Axis air forces in Mediterranean and European skies while often also battling the elements and military bureaucracy. My thanks, too, to John, a prolific Osprey author with whom I collaborated on a definitive history of the 82nd FG (*ADORIMINI*) that was privately published in 1992, for his assistance and encouragement with this project. And lastly, but certainly not least, to my patient and supportive wife, Marjorie, who did the photo editing for the book and provided its author with considerable moral support.

CONTENTS

INTRODUCTION

This is a 'mini' history of one of the USAAF's most successful fighter groups of World War 2, emphasising the exploits of its most successful pilots, particularly its bona fide fighter aces, whose status is defined by scoring a total of five or more officially confirmed aerial victories. Just 26 of the 600+ pilots who served with the 82nd FG during the war met that criteria, 23 of whom achieved 'acedom' whilst actually serving with the group.

Those are not, however, the only 82nd FG pilots who are profiled in these pages. Also included are an even larger number of 'almost' and/or 'strafing' aces, pilots who typically scored three or four confirmed aerial victories plus one or more 'probables', and/or destroyed some enemy aircraft on the ground. These men include many of the unit's flight, squadron and group commanders, who were recipients of the Distinguished Flying Cross (DFC), the Silver Star (SS) and even the Distinguished Service Cross (DSC) for valour in combat and outstanding leadership. They were also 'aces', based on the following definition of that term found in *Webster's Unabridged Dictionary* – 'a very skilled person; expert; adept' – when applied to combat flying in general.

We should not forget when considering the status of aces the importance of luck as well as skill in achieving it, the latter attribute being pretty much a given when it came to America's World War 2 combat pilots. For example, the 82nd did not award credits for shared aerial victories, as did many USAAF fighter groups. Thus, in one case related in these pages, a pilot would not have achieved 'acedom' later had he not won the coin toss for his first, shared, kill. At least three pilots with four confirmed aerial victories ran out of ammunition or had their guns jam while attacking what *could* have been their fifth kill, forcing them to settle for at most a 'probable' or a 'damaged' – and 'almost an ace' status. And then there were the 90 'probably destroyed' credits awarded to dozens of pilots, of which if just a few more had been confirmed the group would have had several more aces.

These few dozen ace pilots – by both definitions – were largely responsible for the extraordinary success of the 82nd FG. Among the group's many accomplishments were 548 enemy aircraft officially credited as destroyed in the air and three Distinguished Unit Citations, plus the destruction of a tremendous amount of enemy materiel both on the ground and on water (sea) by strafing and dive-bombing, including 176 aircraft, 126 locomotives and nine ships.

This is the story of those extraordinary men.

Steve Blake
Prescott Valley
Arizona, USA
March 2012

TRAINING DAZE

I n June 1941 the US Army Air Corps (USAAC) made available to its qualified young enlisted men (EM) an amazing opportunity. Those who applied for this new programme and passed the requisite tests could be appointed as aviation cadets, and at the successful conclusion of their flight training they would become bona fide military pilots – albeit still as EMs (staff sergeants). The first group began their training in August as members of Class 42-C, and 93 of them duly graduated in March 1942.

These men were assigned initially to the 79th Pursuit Group (PG) at Dale Mabry Field in Florida, but in April they were sent to Harding Field, near Baton Rouge, Louisiana, to join the new 82nd PG, which had been activated there in February. The 82nd was comprised of the 95th, 96th and 97th Pursuit Squadrons (PS).

Almost immediately, the group's new staff sergeant pilots, along with its small cadre of officers and non-flying enlisted men, were transferred again, from Harding Field to the Muroc Lake Bombing and Gunnery Range in the Mojave Desert, east of Los Angeles. There, these novice aviators were to be taught to fly the 'hottest' pursuit aeroplane of the newly created US Army Air Forces (USAAF), the high-flying twin-engined Lockheed P-38 Lightning.

Shortly after its arrival at Muroc, the 82nd PG received an infusion of officer pilots and groundcrewmen from the P-38-equipped 1st PG, which was also based in southern California, and was responsible for its air defence. These new pilots were assigned leadership positions – as group, squadron and flight commanders – in the 82nd. They included Capts Harley C Vaughn and Robert E Kirtley. Vaughn, who within a year would be one of the group's first aces, was originally a 97th PS flight leader and its operations officer, but in July he was given command of the 96th. Bob Kirtley was made CO of the 95th PS, effective 1 May.

Two of Kirtley's flight leaders and fellow 1st PG transferees, T H McArthur (who used initials in place of his first and middle names) and Ernest K Osher, were also future aces. The 97th's CO was Capt Ernest C Young. Lt Col William E Covington Jr, formerly a squadron commander in the 1st PG, was initially the 82nd's deputy CO and he then became its CO, effective 17 June.

In mid-May the 82nd, its sergeant pilots' transition to the Lightning complete, was transferred to the Los Angeles area, taking the place of the 1st Fighter Group (FG

95th FS CO Capt Bob Kirtley (holding a model of a B-17) helps his pilots brush up on their aircraft identification at Mines Field. The staff sergeant on the far right, John Litchfield, commanded the 97th FS in Italy in early 1944 as a captain (*Kirtley*)

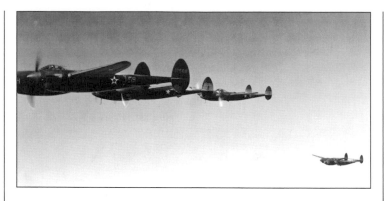

A flight of 95th FS Lightnings over southern California. The second aeroplane, P-38E 41-2092 ('43'), is being flown by future ace SSgt William J Schildt (*Schildt*)

– the USAAF had changed the unit designation Pursuit to Fighter effective 15 May), which was then on its way to the East Coast en route to England and, eventually, North Africa. The 95th FS moved to Mines Field, the 96th to the Grand Central Air Terminal in Glendale and the 97th to Long Beach Airport to continue their training syllabus. Group Headquarters was located initially in downtown Los Angeles and then, in August, joined the 96th FS at Glendale.

After moving to 'LA' the 82nd also received a few junior officer pilots from the 55th FG in Washington State. They included Phillip Rodgers (usually referred to by his initials, P D) and Jack G Walker, who were assigned to the 96th and the 97th FSs, respectively.

Capt Kirtley, in his assigned P-38E 41-2223 ('40'), leads the 95th FS on a training flight along the southern California coast near Malibu. This photograph was taken from a twin-engined A-20 bomber (*Schildt*)

Ten 95th FS sergeant pilots pose for the camera at Mines Field in June 1942. Only five of them would go overseas with the group three months later, two having been killed in flying accidents and three having transferred out. One of the transferees, Claud Ford (in the front row, peering over the shoulders of Alex Hamric, on his right, and Charles Langdon), rejoined the 95th in North Africa a year later. He and Bill Schildt (second from the right) would become aces, with five and six victories, respectively, whilst Hamric would score four, Langdon two and Archie Mallette (in the middle at the top) one. Ford succeeded John Litchfield as CO of the 97th FS in April 1944 and rose in rank from staff sergeant to major in two years! (*Kirtley*)

In early September orders were cut for the group's move to the East Coast, from where it too would ship out for the British Isles. The original plan was for its pilots to fly their Lightnings across the Atlantic, as the 1st and 14th FGs had done earlier that summer, but by the middle of September, when most of the 82nd's personnel boarded a train for New Jersey, that route was closed. It was at this time that the remaining sergeant pilots learned that they had been commissioned as second lieutenants.

Only 38 of the group's original 93 staff sergeant pilots went to Britain with it. Seven of them had been killed in accidents and many more transferred to other stateside units. Most of the latter also served overseas eventually, in every major theatre of war. Eight of them were sent to Guadalcanal in the South Pacific, whilst a dozen others were assigned to fly P-38s to Alaska, three of whom remained there to serve with the squadron they had helped supply with aircraft. Five of the transferees ended up back with the 82nd FG in North Africa and Italy. Of the group's 43 former staff sergeant pilots who did serve with it overseas, eight would become bona fide fighter aces.

A ninth 42-C enlisted pilot also achieved that status. Samuel J Wicker, one of the transferees, was assigned to the new 364th FG in California the following year. The 364th joined the Eighth Air Force in England in early 1944 and Wicker subsequently scored seven confirmed kills, flying P-38s and P-51s.

The group's personnel began boarding the ocean liner *Queen Mary* in New York Harbour on 23 September 1942. Four days later they sailed for the British Isles, the vessel arriving at Greenock, in Scotland, on 3 October. The men of the 82nd FG were transferred to two smaller ships, which took them back across the Irish Sea to Belfast, Northern Ireland. There, they boarded trains to their temporary new home, the RAF airfield at Eglinton, a few miles from Londonderry – the 97th FS was actually based at a satellite field near the town of Maydown. They were now in an actual theatre of war, assigned temporarily to the Eighth Air Force.

It would be more than a month before the 82nd received its new Lightnings. In the meantime the RAF loaned the group some aircraft – including a few examples of the famous Spitfire – so that its pilots could sharpen their flying skills in the interim. Also, RAF veterans lectured them on combat flying in the European Theatre, and radio procedures there. The first of the 82nd's P-38s – F- and G-models – finally arrived on 13 November, and by the end of the month there were about 75 of them on the Irish airfields (the final total was 98).

Inevitably, the American pilots challenged their RAF counterparts to a friendly aerial 'duel', Lightning versus Spitfire. According to Fred J Wolfe, one of the 96th FS's former sergeant pilots, 'Maj Vaughn [recently promoted] went up in a P-38 and a "Limey" went up in a Spitfire and they had a dogfight over the field. Vaughn whipped him and we really razzed the "Limeys"'.

A few new pilots were assigned to the group in Ireland, including three future aces – Ward A Kuentzel, Edward T Waters and Thomas A White. White had originally served with the Royal Canadian Air Force (RCAF) and, like hundreds of other Americans in the RAF and RCAF, had recently transferred to the USAAF.

The Allied invasion of Northwest Africa (Operation *Torch*) had begun on 8 November 1942, shortly after which the 1st and 14th FGs were sent there from England. Both had suffered heavy losses of pilots and aircraft by the end of December, when the 82nd was scheduled to reinforce them. Just before the group left for North Africa, its remaining P-38s that had not already been modified for service there were delivered to Lockheed's Langford Lodge Air Depot, also in Northern Ireland, for that purpose. On 16 December, a large formation of Lightnings flew to St Eval, in Cornwall, on the first leg of their trip. Other smaller formations would make the two-and-a-half-hour flight from Northern Ireland to Cornwall over the next eight days. In the meantime, the first flight to the 82nd FG's new base in Algeria was scheduled for 23 December.

These 95th FS P-38s are being modified for operations in North Africa at the Langford Lodge Air Depot in Northern Ireland just before the group moved to Algeria. Among other things, they received the yellow outlines around the national insignia that all USAAF aeroplanes in the MTO displayed for recognition purposes until the summer of 1943. The 95th was still using individual aircraft numbers, but that would change after it arrived in North Africa. The aircraft in the foreground, P-38F-15 43-2102, was assigned to Verne Yahne, who later named it *Sweet Marie*. This Lightning had a long career with the group before it was destroyed in a crash-landing on 24 May 1944. Lt Yahne completed his combat tour in August 1943 with a score of one enemy aircraft destroyed, one probably destroyed and one damaged (*USAF*)

NORTH AFRICAN AIR WAR

T he first contingent of 51 82nd FG Lightnings began taking off from St Eval at around 0400 hrs on 23 December 1942. It would be an eight-hour-plus flight requiring the utilisation of two 165-gallon auxiliary fuel tanks. Their destination was Tafaroui, a French airfield near Oran, in Algeria. To avoid enemy radar and possible interception, pilots were instructed to fly no more than 200 ft above the surface of the Atlantic. A twin-engined B-26 Marauder led each of the four individual formations and handled most of the navigation.

Since their support personnel would not be joining them for a while, the Lightning pilots had to utilise their aeroplanes as transports, stuffing as many items as they could into every available nook and cranny. To create more space, many of the pilots disconnected their cannon drums and reduced the amount of 0.50-cal ammunition they carried.

As this was a transfer flight, not a combat mission, and it was flown at low level far out from the German-occupied French coast, the possibility of encountering enemy aircraft was not seriously considered. However, as the 95th FS formation approached the middle of the Bay of Biscay, it was attacked by a quartet of twin-engined Ju 88 fighters of 14./KG 40. The German aircraft took them by surprise and quickly shot down a Douglas A-20 Havoc medium bomber that was 'tagging along' to North Africa, as well as the 'tail-end Charlie' P-38, the pilot of which was killed. Bob Kirtley – who had been promoted to major the previous week – described what happened;

'I was sipping tomato juice from a canteen and eating crackers. I had my volume high on "D" Channel and hadn't heard a sound for two hours. The call of "A-20 on fire!" woke me up. I dropped my crackers and spilled my tomato juice in a mad scramble to charge my guns – 50 rounds per 0.50-cal, no 20 mm – firewall rpm and throttle until detonation set in and break toward the A-20, in that order.'

By this time both the Havoc and the P-38 were in the water, and all but one of the Ju 88s had re-entered the cloud cover out of which they had emerged. The pilot of the one remaining German fighter still visible was the one who had shot down the Lightning, and he was evidently hoping to do the same to another – at least until he saw Maj Kirtley's flight turning toward him. He too then pulled up into the overcast, followed by the P-38s.

'As I came out of the overcast I was dead astern of the Ju 88 and closing fast', Kirtley continued. 'At 100 yards I fired one burst – 50 rounds per gun. His left engine exploded, pieces came off and he levelled out right on top of the overcast. I throttled back and flew formation with the aircraft for a minute or so, having exhausted my ammo. He re-entered the overcast, straight and level, and I followed him down. He hit the sea in a nose-down position and came apart'. Bob Kirtley had scored the 82nd FG's first aerial victory (the element leader in his flight shot down another Ju 88 shortly thereafter).

Few of the group's pilots actually made it to Tafaroui that day due to poor weather, although most of them had done so by the 26th, after landing and laying over at Gibraltar or airfields in Morocco. Meanwhile, the group flew its first official combat missions – two uneventful convoy cover patrols – from Tafaroui on Christmas Day. Its temporary new airfield, appropriately nicknamed 'Gooey' Tafaroui, was cold and muddy and had little in the way of amenities. As if the pilots were not depressed enough at that point, they were then given some really bad news. They had to turn over half of their P-38s to the 1st and 14th FGs to help replace their losses of the past two months.

Happily, the 82nd's stay at Tafaroui was brief. Most of the group's remaining pilots flew down from England on 30 December, and after the requisitioned aircraft had been delivered to the 1st and 14th FGs, they all moved again, to Telergma, which was also in Algeria, but farther east and closer to the action, on New Year's Day. It turned out that Telergma, an old Foreign Legion outpost, was even more isolated and its facilities just as primitive as Tafaroui's.

The group's primary mission in North Africa was to escort medium bombers – North American B-25 Mitchells and Martin B-26 Marauders. Due to the group now having only half of its authorised number of Lightnings, the 82nd's remaining aeroplanes were placed into a pool and then, according to their availability, assigned to pilots scheduled for missions. This situation would continue until the 82nd finally received some replacement aircraft in February 1943.

For an escort of B-26s of the 319th Bomb Group (BG), which was also based at Telergma, on 7 January, the 96th FS's 2Lt William J Sloan (a former staff sergeant pilot) was assigned P-38F-15 43-2112 of the 95th FS. Sloan, who was from Virginia, had acquired the nickname 'Dixie' because of his pronounced Southern drawl. It was during this mission that the 82nd FG had its first contact with enemy aircraft over North Africa. Near the target – Gabes, in Tunisia – six Bf 109s attacked the formation. Lt Sloan hit one of them, which was seen to crash. By an interesting coincidence, the group's first victory in North Africa had been claimed by what were to be its top-scoring pilot and P-38.

Another future ace, 2Lt Tom White of the 97th FS, scored his first kill the day after Sloan's near Kairouan, in Tunisia, also during a B-26 escort whilst flying P-38F-5 42-12641. Having been attacked by an Fw 190, White quickly turned the tables and fired a long burst into the fighter and then saw it crash.

The 96th FS flew a tough mission on 15 January. It was another Marauder escort, this time to the bridges at Oued El Akarit, in Tunisia. The fight that ensued resulted in the loss of two P-38s to Bf 109 pilots of II./JG 51. Maj Vaughn began his scoring that day with a confirmed victory. Three other Bf 109s were credited as probably destroyed, one of them to 2Lt Fred Wolfe, whose victim had just killed one of his best friends, whom he watched going down in flames.

On the 17th, during an anti-shipping B-25 escort by the 97th FS, some hostile twin-engined aircraft were spotted near Sicily and three were

Lt Tom White of the 97th FS scored his first victory – and the group's second over North Africa – on 8 January 1943 when he shot down an Fw 190 near Kairouan, in Tunisia. His given middle name was Ace, and in less than two months he would achieve the status to match it (*Jack Cook*)

shot down. A Ju 88 was credited to the squadron's new CO, Capt William W Wittliff, while Capt William B 'Pete' Petersen (who, like Wittliff, had transferred to the 82nd from the 1st PG in California) and former sergeant pilot and future ace 2Lt Herman W Visscher each claimed a single Ju 52/3m transport apiece.

Four days later the group escorted the Marauders on another anti-shipping assignment. The formation, including ten P-38s of the 96th and 97th FSs, was near Cap Bon when the bombers attacked an enemy convoy. As the Lightning pilots monitored a nearby Axis airfield they saw sand swirls and knew fighters (which they soon identified as Bf 109s) were being scrambled to intercept them. When the Messerschmitt pilots had gained sufficient altitude they attacked, shooting down two of the 97th's aeroplanes. The pilots of these machines were avenged by their squadronmates, who claimed four of the Bf 109s destroyed, one of which was Tom White's second victory.

Around the same time, two Italian three-engined bombers were spotted. They were escorted by a handful of fighters identified as Bf 109s and Fw 190s, but which were in fact Macchi C.202s. In this, the 82nd's first encounter with the *Regia Aeronautica*, the bombers were shot down by 2Lts Charles J Zubarik (96th) and Lloyd E Atteberry (97th), both of whom were former staff sergeant pilots. Zubarik, who was called either 'Ricky' or 'Shorty' by his squadronmates, also accounted for one of the fighters. He was officially credited with a 'Ju 52' and an 'Fw 190', whilst Atteberry's victim was identified as a 'Cant Z.1007', although the tri-motors were actually Savoia-Marchetti SM.84s.

On 29 January the 95th and 96th FSs escorted B-25s and B-26s to the El Aouina airfield near Tunis, home to the Luftwaffe's JG 53, whose pilots attacked them. The P-38 pilots claimed two Bf 109s destroyed, two probably destroyed and two damaged without loss in that action. The confirmed kills were credited to 1Lt Ernie Osher and former sergeant pilot 2Lt Claude R Kinsey Jr of the 95th and 96th, respectively – the first claims by these future aces. The probable victories were scored by Capt T H McArthur and 2Lt Bill Schildt (in P-38G-5 42-12806). Within three months these two 95th FS pilots would also be aces.

The following morning the 96th FS escorted the Mitchells to El Aouinet, near Gabes. Bf 109s of II./JG 51 attacked as the bombers approached their target over the sea, initiating a particularly hard-fought air battle. No bombers were lost, but three P-38 pilots were missing in action and 'Ricky' Zubarik had to crash-land his Lightning in a field after losing both of his engines. In return, the 96th was credited with eight kills and two probables. Amongst those claiming single victories were Maj Vaughn and 2Lts Kinsey, Sloan and Wolfe (Kinsey also scored a probable).

On the morning of the last day of January the 95th FS escorted the B-26s on another anti-shipping strike, during which two Bf 110s of III./ZG 26 were shot down by Capt McArthur and 2Lt Schildt (once

The 97th FS's Lt Herman Visscher scored the first of his eventual five victories on 17 January 1943 when he shot down a Ju 52/3m transport. He is pictured here with his P-38 in March of that year, by which time he was credited with the two confirmed kills displayed on the fighter's nose, plus two probables (*Wallace Reyerson*)

The 96th FS's Lt Charles 'Ricky' Zubarik and his P-38 *Pearl* (serial number unknown), which he named after his mother, shortly after scoring his first two victories on 21 January 1943. This was probably the aircraft he crash-landed at the completion of yet another mission eight days later (*Claude Kinsey*)

again in 42-12806). Meanwhile, eight P-38s of the 97th FS, together with a squadron from the 1st FG, accompanied some other B-26s to Gabes airfield. Two of the 97th's pilots aborted and the other two members of their flight became separated from the rest of the formation, leaving just the four-aeroplane flight led by Tom White, which was attacked by Bf 109s of JG 53. Three of these Lightnings and another from the 1st FG were shot down. Lt White, his flight's sole survivor, made the only USAAF claim, for a Bf 109 destroyed – his third victory. He described what happened in his report;

'On our way home from the target, I spotted two enemy aircraft about to attack from behind. I made a full 180-degree turn and fired a long burst at full deflection into one Me 109 as he veered off. Smoke poured from the engine cowling and flame came from the right-hand side of the fuselage. The Me 109 crashed into the ground close behind a P-38 that had just crashed there.'

The group finally received some reinforcements in early February, after the two-squadron 14th FG had been withdrawn from the front at the end of January to reorganise. The 14th's surviving original pilots were sent home and the replacements that joined it in Algeria were transferred to the 82nd, as were some of its remaining P-38s. Also, later that month replacement aircraft began to be sent from England to both the 1st and 82nd FGs.

The group's first action in February came on the 2nd, during another anti-shipping escort. Sixteen 96th FS P-38s were shepherding six B-26s when the Marauders attacked a convoy near Cap Bon. Two-dozen enemy aircraft of various types were encountered over and near the convoy, of which the Lightning pilots claimed seven destroyed, one probable and two damaged. Some Bf 109s tried to break through to the bombers and three of them were shot down for their efforts. There were also some Italian aeroplanes in the area, including several three-engined Cant Z.506 flying boats, two of which were downed by 2Lts William B Rawson (a former sergeant pilot whose nickname was 'Hut-sut', after a popular song) and P D Rodgers, who in addition damaged two of the Bf 109s.

'Dixie' Sloan had a particularly eventful day, scoring his third and fourth victories. The P-38 pilots went into a protective Lufbery Circle whilst defending the Marauders. One of the Bf 109s that attempted to get at the bombers by breaking through the circle was foiled by Lt Sloan, who was set up

'Dixie' Sloan poses with his new P-38F-15 43-2064 shortly after scoring his third and fourth victories on 2 February 1943, the Lightning he was flying on that occasion having been badly shot up by an Fw 190. He has not yet had the name *Snooks* (his nickname for his wife, Shirley) painted on the P-38. Lt Sloan scored his fifth victory on 15 February, most likely in this aeroplane, to become the 82nd FG's first ace (*Smithsonian*)

almost perfectly for a shot and had only to roll out slightly to get off an accurate burst, whereupon the Messerschmitt exploded in midair.

When the returning 96th pilots reached the coast an Fw 190 came out of nowhere, slipped behind Sloan's aeroplane, opened fire and then just as quickly departed. Amongst other things it shot up one of his engines and damaged his right vertical stabiliser to the extent that it was only held in place by the control cables. Also, hydraulic fluid was spraying into the cockpit, covering Sloan's goggles and obscuring his vision. The P-38 was, however, still flyable – barely. Sloan moved under the nearby B-26 formation to procure some protection. With one engine out, his hydraulic system gone, the wind whistling through his cockpit and a vertical stabiliser that could come off at any moment, Lt Sloan was ready to call it a day. But then a twin-engined Do 217 attacked the Marauders. Despite his fighter's fragile condition, 'Dixie' slipped beneath the Dornier, fired, and it went down.

2Lt Paul R Cochran, one of the recent 14th FG transferees, also shot down one of the Bf 109s, for his second victory – this was Cochran's first mission with the 82nd. He had scored his first kill just five days earlier with the 49th FS, on the 14th's last mission before it was relieved.

The following morning the 95th and 97th FSs, together with a squadron from the 1st FG, escorted Marauders to Gabes airfield – such missions were now referred to unofficially as 'Gabes Meat Runs' due to their high risk factor. As the formation approached the field, Bf 109s were seen taking off. They attacked after the bomb run, commencing a long running fight, the results of which were not favourable to the 82nd FG. Three of its pilots were killed (a B-26 was also lost) against claims of one destroyed, two probables and three damaged. The 95th's 2Lt Wilbur S 'Will' Hattendorf – one of the pilots who had transferred to the 82nd in California from the 55th FG – made his first claim in this action, for a Bf 109 damaged. The two probables were credited to Tom White and Herman Visscher of the 97th. The only confirmed kill was by their squadronmate Lloyd Atteberry, who also damaged one. Atteberry described his intense experience a few days later;

'We were just leaving the target when the wingman and I saw four Messerschmitts behind us. I turned back to knock them off the wingman's tail. Of course, the rest of the formation went on. Then in the dogfight that followed, the wingman got separated from me and ran for home. Eventually that's what I did too, but I was too busy for a while. Two were on my tail and I was on the tail of a third. The one I was following attempted to reverse the direction of his turn, and that was when I got him. He blew up right there and went down.'

The other two Bf 109s continued chasing Lt Atteberry down on the deck. 'Every time you go up, you're scared, but this time I was panicky'. He chopped one throttle and spun a turn. When he came out of it he was right above the ground, and then three more Bf 109s joined the chase. 'I thought I was through. I would have bailed out if I had been high enough, but you can't bail out at 15 ft'. Somehow, Atteberry managed to shake off all but one of them. 'Rough air is probably all that kept him from hitting me, and eventually he ran out of ammunition'. His squadronmates dubbed the manoeuvre he used to evade the Bf 109s – chopping the throttle on one engine and cranking in full aileron and rudder on that side – 'The Atteberry Roll'.

The 96th FS flew an anti-shipping escort an hour later and also encountered enemy fighters. As the B-26s attacked two ships some twin-engined aircraft were spotted and three of them subsequently destroyed. Although identified as two 'Me 210s' and a 'Ju 88', they were all in fact Bf 110s of II./ZG 26 that were escorting the ships – three Messerschmitts were recorded as having been lost to P-38s. 2Lt William T Vantrease, another former staff sergeant pilot, was credited with an 'Me 210' and a 'Ju 88'.

On 7 February the 95th and 96th FSs participated in the first Twelfth Air Force bombing raid on Sardinia. Lt Wolfe and Maj Vaughn each claimed a Bf 109, the former's being credited as destroyed and the latter's as a probable.

The following day the 82nd FG flew its most successful mission to date – another 'Gabes Meat Run' by the 97th FS, escorting Mitchells and Marauders. The Lightning pilots, tied to the bombers, watched as 24 Bf 109s from JGs 51 and 77 rose to greet them. When the smoke cleared, eight German fighters were claimed as having been shot down and two more damaged. Scoring single confirmed kills were Capt Petersen and 2Lts Lloyd Atteberry, Gerald L Rounds and Herman Visscher. Former sergeant pilot Gerry Rounds recalled;

2Lt Bill Vantrease is seen in the cockpit of 'Dixie' Sloan's 43-2064 shortly after claiming his first two victories on 3 February 1943 (*USAF*)

Fred Wolfe scored the second of his four kills during the first USAAF raid on Sardinia on 7 February 1943. Here, Wolfe poses with his P-38, 'BH' (serial number unknown), and its groundcrew. The latter are, from left to right, Sgt Rex Ortmann, TSgt Cash Bowen (crew chief), Lt Wolfe and Sgt John Smith (*Wolfe*)

Former staff sergeant pilot and future ace Lt Gerry Rounds scored the first of his five confirmed victories (all Bf 109s) during a 'Gabes Meat Run' on 8 February 1943 (*Rounds*)

'In any direction one looked, there were P-38s and Me 109s diving straight down or going straight up – many in vertical banks, leaving two silver vapour trails from their wingtips. We fought for approximately 20 minutes from 10,000 ft down to zero. There would be a flicker of a '109 – you led him, fired a short burst, and you would see another out of the corner of your eye doing the same thing with you. You'd twist toward him to shorten his firing period, get a burst in if you could, break off your attack and then start in on another that was coming your way. It wasn't at all unusual to see a P-38 firing at a '109, with another '109 on the P-38's tail, as well as a P-38 on *that* '109's tail. But the train would only last a second or two, before breaking up as soon as the situation was realised by those in it.'

At one point Rounds saw a Bf 109 on the tail of another Lightning as he was upside down, viewing the scene through the top of his canopy. He was in a perfect position for a deflection shot, and when he fired the Messerschmitt shed pieces of its canopy, fell away trailing white smoke, and then went into a flaming spin. His first kill!

Part of the secret of the 97th pilots' success that day was that they had previously decided amongst themselves to take the initiative by leaving the bombers and engaging the enemy fighters as soon as they were attacked. Unfortunately, this tactic did not serve the bombers nearly as well, with four 310th BG Mitchells being shot down and two more crash-landing back at their base due to battle damage.

The next notable mission was on 15 February, when the 96th FS escorted 17th BG B-26s to the airfield at Kairouan. The result was two more victories – a Bf 109 to 'Dixie' Sloan and an Fw 190 to Tom White (in P-38G-10 42-12888). This was kill number five for Sloan, making him the group's first ace.

The only real excitement during the next few days took place on the 17th during a B-26 escort to Sardinia by the 96th FS. The mission had in fact been quite uneventful up to the point when Claude Kinsey spotted a Z.506 floatplane flying low over the water on the way home. He dove on it from 9000 ft but lost sight of the Cant due to his excessive speed, forcing him to make a second pass. This time Kinsey hit the floatplane with a good burst and it disintegrated.

21 February found Maj Kirtley leading the 95th FS on another anti-shipping sweep with the Mitchells. He was flying 43-2112, which now displayed on its nose the name and image of *"THE SAD SACK"*, a popular cartoon character of the period. On its outer coolant radiator housings were the large white letters 'AS', 'A' indicating that it was a 95th machine and 'S' being the aeroplane's individual letter within the squadron. The letters 'B' and 'C' identified the 96th and 97th FSs, respectively.

A variety of mostly twin-engined enemy aircraft were encountered over and near the target convoy, and Kirtley moved quickly to counteract the intervention of some Ju 88s. He shot up one that limped off towards Sicily (Kirtley was credited with damaging this machine), then hit another that half-rolled and dove straight into the sea. Next, he spotted what he thought was an Italian floatplane, but it was actually a single-engined German Arado Ar 196, which he literally shot to pieces 50 ft off the surface of the water.

Lt Claude Kinsey with his P-38G-10 *Milly* (42-12871) after scoring his fourth victory on 23 February 1943 (*Kinsey*)

These 96th FS pilots were photographed in front of Claude Kinsey's *Milly* around 1 March 1943. They are, from left to right, Lts Lee H Lawrence, Douglas E Crichton, Kinsey, 'Dixie' Sloan, John Perrone and P D Rodgers. Kinsey and Lawrence (who had one victory) were both shot down on 5 April, the former becoming a PoW whilst the latter was killed. Doug Crichton (with two victories) was killed in action on 3 July (*Kinsey*)

Capt McArthur also led his flight into the Ju 88s, duelling with a gunner in one of them until the weapon fell silent. Soon the Ju 88 succumbed to the P-38's heavy firepower, beginning a wide turn with one engine on fire before diving steeply into the Mediterranean. 2Lt Alex K Hamric also shot down a Ju 88 in this action, the total claims for which were eight destroyed, two probables and one damaged without loss.

Whilst the 96th FS was escorting the 310th BG over the sea shortly after noon on the 22nd, six Ju 88s attacked the Mitchells as they were bombing a convoy northeast of Cap Bon. They succeeded in shooting down one of the bombers but Paul Cochran did the same to the Ju 88 flown by Major Richard Meyer, *Gruppenkommandeur* of II./KG 76, who was killed.

On 23 February, during another sea sweep by the 96th, Claude Kinsey had an experience almost identical to the one six days earlier, once again spotting a lone Z.506 and shooting it down.

The 95th and 97th FSs flew a bomber escort to the railway bridge at La Hencha, in Tunisia, on the 28th. Bf 109s intercepted the formation and the Lightning pilots claimed two destroyed, three probables and two damaged for the loss of a P-38 and its pilot. One of the confirmed kills was credited to Tom White (in P-38G-10 42-12943), who became the group's second ace, as this was his fifth success. By an amazing coincidence, his given middle name was Ace, which was also his nickname! Amongst the other claimants were Bill Schildt (who was flying P-38F-5 42-12612) and Herman Visscher, with a probable each. As of the end of that day the 82nd was the highest-scoring USAAF fighter group in the MTO, despite its late arrival in-theatre.

The group began March eventfully on the 1st. That afternoon the 96th and 97th FSs returned to La Hencha with the 17th BG, the latter squadron providing close support and the former top cover. As the formation approached the target, two flights of Bf 109s attacked, boring straight through the top cover to the B-26s and shooting down two of them. Unfortunately, only two of the close-cover P-38s remained to protect the bombers, the rest having aborted. The remaining duo – 2Lts Ray Crawford and Gerry Rounds – tackled the Bf 109s and broke up their attack. Crawford downed two of them in the process and Rounds one. Lt Crawford, who was one of the 14th FG transferees, recalled this mission several months later;

'One of the B-26s, crippled by flak, fell behind. An Me 109 dived right past us and made a pass at this bomber, then started back into the sun, with Rounds on his tail. Rounds got him. Then a second '109 roared in for a thrust, but I was in a good position. Spinning right into him, I let him have it. As I climbed back toward the bombers, I looked over my shoulder and saw the Jerry pilot bailing out.

Jack Walker poses next to the group scoreboard on 8 March 1943 – the day after his first victory. His is the last name in the third (97th FS) column (*Walker*)

A third '109 dived at us almost immediately. I repeated my previous procedure and, as I raced the Jerry back into the sun, I discovered that the Lightning definitely out-flies the Messerschmitt. I fired away and saw him crash in smoke.'

Meanwhile, the top-cover pilots were also busy. Just before the target they lost the B-26s in thick cloud, and when the Marauders emerged the Bf 109s attacked, downing two of them. The 96th then waded in, claiming two German fighters destroyed (by 2Lts John A Perrone and P D Rodgers) and four damaged.

On 7 March the 97th FS escorted B-25s on another sea sweep. A mixture of German and Italian aircraft were encountered near the targeted convoy, and the result was claims for four destroyed and three damaged without loss to the Americans. 2Lt Jack Walker scored his first victory by shooting down a Z.506 seaplane. He recalled years later that he and Capt 'Pete' Petersen 'were startled to see this three-engined Cant Z. Petersen said "Hey! Hey!" and banked to the right. I banked right behind him. He shot behind and I shot in front. I got her and she just crumpled'. Petersen shot down a Ju 88 a short while later, whilst Capt Wittliff destroyed another Junkers 'twin' and a C.200 fighter.

Four days later the 97th was back in action against the Luftwaffe whilst escorting B-26s over the sea to attack some ships. Two Me 210s from III./ZG 1 intervened and managed to shoot down one of the Marauders before they were in turn downed by 'Ace' White (for his sixth victory) and Lloyd Atteberry (for his fourth). Another anti-shipping sweep was flown the very next day (12 March), this time by the 96th FS and some B-25s. Two Italian bombers were spotted and shot down by Maj Vaughn and Lt Ed 'Shorty' Waters. Although identified as Cant Z.1007s, they were in fact SM.84s.

It was back to a Tunisian target on the 15th, when the whole group, plus Spitfires of the 31st FG, escorted B-26s to Mezzouna airfield. The mission was relatively uneventful until a handful of Bf 109s ripped through the formation on the way home and shot down one of the P-38s. The Lightning pilots initially thought the Messerschmitts were Spitfires, and were therefore caught off guard. They quickly gathered their wits and retaliated, claiming one destroyed, one probably destroyed (by Claude Kinsey) and one damaged.

The 82nd FG flew a particularly successful mission on 20 March when the 96th and 97th FSs escorted B-25s of the newly arrived 321st BG on an anti-shipping assignment. The 97th became separated from the rest of the formation when they chased after some enemy aircraft that proved impossible to catch. Meanwhile, the Mitchells attacked a convoy and set a large freighter on fire, but they spent so long over the enemy vessels that an estimated 50 Axis aircraft had time to come to the ships' assistance from Sicily, resulting in a huge air battle for the 96th.

This fight produced claims for 11 destroyed, one probable and one damaged. The top scorer, with two Bf 109 kills, was 2Lt 'Ricky' Zubarik, who was flying his new Lightning (P-38G-10 42-13054/'BS'), which he had christened *Pearl III*. Amongst those claiming single Bf 109s destroyed were 2Lts Joseph Wayne Jorda (another of the group's ex-sergeant pilots, who went by his middle name) in P-38G-10 42-13042, Ward Kuentzel (in P-38F-15 43-2153), 'Hut-sut' Rawson (in P-38G-10 42-13016) and P D Rodgers (in P-38G-15 43-2318). Maj Vaughn (in P-38G-5 42-12827) shot down one of the two Ju 88s claimed in this action, whilst 2Lt Claude Kinsey (at the controls of his P-38G-10 42-12871, named *Milly*) was credited with the only Italian aircraft destroyed – an unidentified single-engined fighter. This was Kinsey's fifth confirmed kill, thus making him the 82nd FG's third ace. Although no P-38s were lost, two of the B-25s were shot down.

Two hours later, the 95th FS was involved in a brief dogfight with some Bf 109s near the Tebaga landing ground northwest of Gabes during a B-26 escort that resulted in claims for three probably destroyed, one of which was 2Lt Daniel F Sharp's first success.

22 March turned out to be another big day for the group when 38 Lightnings of the 95th and 97th FSs escorted 15 B-26s of the 17th BG on a sea sweep. The first attack came near Cap Serrat, two Bf 109s of I./JG 53 making a quick pass at the 95th FS and sending one of its Lightnings crashing into the sea. Shortly thereafter, two-dozen more hit both the P-38s and the B-26s. Although they succeeded in downing one of the bombers, the German fighters could not prevent two ships from being sunk, or two of their own from being shot down. During the withdrawal, the 82nd's pilots found themselves in a running battle as more enemy aircraft joined the fight. Seven additional Bf 109s were claimed destroyed, plus three probables and two damaged, against the loss of two more P-38s. One of the latter was flown by 2Lt Lloyd Atteberry, who, with four victories to his credit, was one of the 97th FS's most successful pilots. Last seen going into a loop with a Bf 109, Atteberry was eventually declared Killed in Action.

Maj Kirtley scored his fourth, and last, confirmed victory in this fight, flying P-38G-10 42-13049. Amongst the other claimants were Capt McArthur (a probable), Capt Osher (a destroyed and a damaged), Lt Sharp (his first confirmed kill) and Lt Crawford (a probable). Will Hattendorf made his second claim, which was credited to him as a probable. He was flying his new P-38F-15, 43-2181/'AY', which he had named *My Baby* after his wife.

The 25th brought yet another – in this case ill-fated – anti-shipping mission. After an enemy seaplane was spotted and shot down, the formation was scattered by exceptionally strong winds and the pilots had to find their way home as best they could. The group suffered the loss of

96th FS CO Maj Harley Vaughn and his first *TWIN ENGIN INJUN* Lightning (believed to be P-38G-5 42-12827), which displays two victory symbols. He scored his third kill on 12 March when he despatched a German bomber into the sea. The aeroplane's colourful name and artwork were evidently inspired by the Native Americans in his home state, Oklahoma (*Col Ray Toliver*)

Six 97th FS pilots pose with Herman Visscher's P-38. They are, from left to right, Lts Emory Claude Morgan, Merle E 'Swede' Larson, Justin O 'Joe' Henley, Tom White, Visscher and Lloyd Atteberry, who was killed in action on 22 March 1943, not long after this photograph was taken. White was already an ace and Visscher would finally achieve that status five months later, whilst the other men scored one, three, two and four confirmed victories, respectively (*Morgan*)

Some 95th FS officers enjoy their rest leave in early April 1943 while staying at a luxury hotel on the Mediterranean shore at Agadir, in Morocco. The group's pilots normally received such R&R about halfway through their 50-mission combat tours. They are, from left to right, Lts Verne Yahne, Archie 'Muscles' Mallette and Jesse 'Blackie' Oliver and Capt T H McArthur. When he returned from his leave on 12 April, McArthur became the new squadron CO and then scored single victories on the 17th, 28th and 29th to become an ace. He was killed in a tragic accident on 3 May. The other three men completed their tours unharmed, with a single confirmed victory apiece (*P D Rodgers*)

one of its aces when 2Lt Tom White crash-landed at Telergma due to an engine failure. His P-38 ended up upside down, with its canopy jammed against the ground. 'Ace' had to shoot his way out of a side window with his 0.45-cal pistol! Badly injured, he was taken to hospital, bringing his combat tour to a premature end after just 22 missions. White recovered from his injuries and subsequently flew another P-38 tour in England with the Eighth Air Force's 55th FG.

On 28 March the 82nd FG began the move to its new base, Berteaux, which was 12 miles east of Telergma and even more desolate. It was completed four days later.

The 95th and 96th FSs flew another sea sweep with the B-25s on the 31st. A Ju 88 was encountered and shot down, but then the formation was bounced by some Bf 109s, which downed two of the 95th's P-38s and two B-25s. One of the former was credited to Feldwebel Bernhard Schneider of 5./JG 27 as his 20th victory. In return, 2Lt Marion 'Manny' Moore claimed to have shot down one of the Messerschmitts.

Bob Kirtley left the group on 1 April, having flown his 24th, and last, mission with the 95th FS on 25 March. After leave at a rest camp, he was assigned to the Fighter Replacement Training Center (FRTC) at Berrechid, near Casablanca, as chief P-38 instructor. In June Kirtley was given command of a new P-38 unit (later designated the 449th FS) made up of recent FRTC graduates and veterans of the 1st and 82nd FGs that was being organised for service in China. When the squadron left for the Far East the following month, Maj Kirtley was reassigned again, this time to his original unit, the 1st FG, with which he completed his combat tour. He added a probable and a damaged claim with the 1st, bringing his total to four destroyed, two probables and one damaged.

Following Kirtley's departure on 1 April, 1Lt Alex Hamric temporarily assumed command of the 95th until Capt McArthur returned from rest camp and officially became its new CO on 12 April.

The constant attacks on the ships attempting to re-supply and reinforce their armies in Tunisia had left the Axis in desperate straits, so they decided to supply their troops (and later evacuate some of them) increasingly by transport aircraft from Sicily. The Allied fighter patrols sent up to intercept these flights, commencing officially on 5 April, were given the code name Operation *Flax*.

The 82nd FG participated in four of the subsequent slaughters of Axis transport aeroplanes. The first, on the 5th, was not actually a *Flax* mission but rather a typical sea sweep by the 96th and 97th FSs with the B-25s north of Cap Bon. They rendezvoused with the 1st FG over an Axis ship convoy at 0820 hrs, and shortly thereafter a large aerial formation came into view, headed for Tunis. The 82nd's pilots waded into the 30+ transports, while the escorting Bf 109s of II./JG 27 attacked them in turn, attempting, with limited success, to protect their charges. The P-38 pilots were credited with 17 destroyed (including nine transports), three probables and five damaged, but lost four of their own to the Bf 109s. The 1st FG joined in and was credited with 19 kills (including 11 transports) for the loss of two of its Lightnings.

One of the missing 82nd FG pilots was 1Lt Claude Kinsey. He had led his 96th FS flight into the transports and shot down two of them, which made him, with seven confirmed kills, the highest-scoring P-38 pilot in North Africa. His elation was short-lived, however, as he was himself then shot down by one of the Bf 109s. Kinsey was taken prisoner but managed to escape from captivity in Italy five months later. He then spent another four weeks behind enemy lines before finally meeting up with Allied troops. Kinsey subsequently related what happened on his last mission;

'I just had a chance to set afire two Ju 52s when, "zowie", it felt as though I'd run smack into a brick wall. I was going 350 mph, flying about 50 ft above the waves. I headed her into land and, just by luck, managed to bail out 20 yards off the coast. My ribs were crushed, my legs were injured and I had sustained first- and second-degree burns on my face. Five Arabs pounced on me and carried me piggy-back up a cliff to an Italian prison camp.'

A cannon shell had exploded in Kinsey's left wing tank, and he was able to pull up to just 300 ft before jettisoning his canopy. He bailed out by standing up on the seat and letting the slipstream drag him free of his burning P-38. Kinsey's ribs were crushed by the force of his parachute opening at such a high speed, and he hit the water almost immediately thereafter. With his legs so badly injured that they were virtually useless, Kinsey had to struggle through waist-deep water to make it to the beach. His leather gloves and helmet had protected his hands and his head from more serious burns (the helmet was almost completely burned away).

The top-scoring 82nd FG pilot in this action was 2Lt Merle E 'Swede' Larson of the 97th FS, with two Ju 52/3ms and an Me 210 destroyed – his only confirmed kills. Amongst the other claimants were his squadronmates 1Lt Jack Walker (a Ju 52/3m destroyed and a Ju 88 damaged) and 2Lt Ray Crawford (a Bf 109 destroyed). The 96th's scorers included 2Lt Paul Cochran (a Bf 109 destroyed), 1Lt Wayne Jorda (two

Ju 52/3ms destroyed plus an Fw 190 damaged) and 1Lt Bill 'Hut-sut' Rawson (one Bf 109 destroyed and three more damaged).

Later that month Jack Walker became ill and was sent to hospital. When he was discharged in May, he was sent on a Temporary Duty attachment to instruct French Air Force pilots on the Bell P-39 Airacobra. Walker finally returned to the 97th FS to complete his combat tour in mid-October.

The 95th FS escorted some Mitchells to Sicily later on the morning of the 5th. As they left the target, enemy fighters attacked and a 30-minute running fight ensued, during which a C.200 was claimed destroyed by Lt Hamric and a Bf 109 downed by Lt Hattendorf in *My Baby*.

Five days later, on 10 April, 27 P-38s of the 95th and 97th FSs were escorting B-25s on a sweep between Cap Rosa and Cap Bizerte shortly after noon when another large formation of enemy aircraft – including about 30 transports – was spotted and immediately attacked. Alex Hamric led the 95th into them and quickly shot down a Ju 52/3m. By the end of the action, he and his squadronmates had claimed seven destroyed and two damaged for the loss of one P-38. The 97th also waded in and claimed five more transports, including two to Ray Crawford. These gave him a total of five confirmed victories, so the group had a new ace.

Then, according to the mission report, 'After the P-38s had left the transports, at least seven of which were seen burning on the surface of the water, 15 Me 109s appeared from Bizerte at 1250 hrs'. These fighters made desperate attempts to attack the Mitchells, but they were fended off successfully by the Lightning pilots. Bill Schildt (in P-38F-15 43-2082) managed to down one of the Bf 109s, which was seen to crash into the sea near Bizerte, and three others were damaged.

The 82nd FG's earlier successes that month were only preliminaries to its big score on 11 April, which resulted from two *Flax* missions. The first was flown by the 95th FS, which took off shortly after 0600 hrs. Ten miles off the west coast of Sicily near Marsala, 20 Ju 52/3ms, with

The 95th's Lt Bill Schildt was assigned this P-38G-15 (43-2406), which he named *CAT SASS*, in late April 1943. He crash-landed his previous aircraft, 43-2082, at Bône, in Algeria, after the squadron's hugely successful combat on the 11th of that month, during which he shot down three Ju 52/3ms to become an ace. Schildt scored his sixth, and last, victory with 43-2406 on 14 May (*Schildt*)

an escort of Bf 109s, Bf 110s and Ju 88s, were sighted heading south. Alex Hamric, who was leading the 95th again, sent a Ju 52/3m down in bright orange flames and black smoke on his first pass – it soon became apparent that the transports were carrying gasoline. He then downed another. Bill Schildt, one of the other flight leaders (once again at the controls of 43-2082), flamed three more Ju 52/3ms. These gave him a total of five kills, making him the group's fifth ace. 'Manny' Moore had shot down one and was making a pass at another when it skidded to get out of his way and crashed into the sea without him having fired a shot. He downed a Bf 109 as well. 2Lt John R Meyer, another former sergeant pilot, also shot down three Ju 52/3ms – his only aerial victories. A total of 18 transports were claimed destroyed by the 95th FS pilots.

The squadron's remaining two flights provided cover for their comrades who were devastating the transports below them. 2Lt Danny Sharp was particularly successful, damaging a Bf 110 and then targeting another. However, the gunner of the latter machine managed to shoot out one of Sharp's engines before his Bf 110 went down. Despite having only a single operable engine, Sharp still managed to get behind a Bf 109 and destroy it too. 2Lt Will Hattendorf, in *My Baby*, shot down a Ju 88 and a Bf 110, 2Lt Thomas D Hodgson claimed one Ju 88 destroyed and another probably destroyed and 2Lt Robert W Muir was also credited with a probable Junkers 'twin'.

The credits for this mission totalled 27 destroyed, six probables and one damaged. Seven pilots scored multiple victories. The 82nd FG's most successful single aerial engagement of the war was not without loss, however. Three of its pilots were killed, including 1Lt Hamric, who had just scored his fourth victory. Having also had an engine shot out, Hamric made it as far as Galite Island before he simply disappeared, having evidently crashed into the sea. III./ZG 26 claimed seven(!) P-38s destroyed, four of them being credited to Leutnant Paul Bley, for the loss of two of its Bf 110s and their crews.

The 96th FS flew a similar mission later that morning, Lt 'Hut-sut' Rawson's flight shooting down five more Ju 52/3ms. Unfortunately, 'Hut-sut' was killed in this action, Fred Wolfe, a close friend, remembering that 'We were on a sea sweep and flying right on the water when "Hut-sut" called in some Ju 52s in front of his flight. I remember him saying "Let's go get 'em". The last his flight saw of him was when he was making a pass on a Ju 52 with one of his engines smoking'.

Rawson downed one of the transports prior to his demise, thus raising his tally to four destroyed, one probable and three damaged. The remaining three members of his flight claimed the following tri-motors destroyed – element leader 2Lt John Perrone got one, Perrone's wingman 2Lt Herman S 'Lee' Solem two and Rawson's wingman, Flt Off Frank Hurlbut, one. Hurlbut and Solem had joined the squadron just nine days earlier, and this was only the former's second combat mission.

The 95th and 96th FSs flew an Operation *Flax* sweep over the Straits of Sicily on 17 April. On the return leg three twin-engined enemy aircraft, identified as Fiat BR.20 bombers, were spotted and quickly shot down by the 96th, the victors including 'Shorty' Waters and John Perrone. Another BR.20 and a Ju 88 then came into view, and they were targeted by the squadron commanders, Capt McArthur and Maj

Lt Bill 'Hut-sut' Rawson, one of the 96th FS's most popular and successful pilots, was killed in action on 11 April 1943 after downing a Ju 52/3m transport. With a final score of four destroyed, one probable and three damaged, there is little doubt that he would have become an ace had he survived longer (*John Bybee*)

Ed 'Shorty' Waters joined the 96th FS in Northern Ireland, and his first claim was for a Bf 109 damaged on 1 March 1943. He then shot down a Cant Z.1007 on 12 March and a BR.20 near Zembra Island on 17 April. This photo of Lt Waters and his P-38G-10 *"MIGHTY MITE"* (a description of its diminutive, but extremely aggressive, pilot) was taken after his third kill, on 20 May, en route to a total of seven. *"MIGHTY MITE's"* serial number is unfortunately not known (*John Gray*)

Lt Richard Kenney scored his first victory in a spectacular manner on 28 April 1943 and performed even more impressively a week later when he shot down two SM.82 transports and a Bf 109 in a single mission. He was himself shot down (by flak) over Sardinia and captured on 15 June, however. Kenney is seen here standing next to the 95th FS's mission board at Souk-el-Arba (*Kenney*)

Vaughn – McArthur shot down the Fiat and Vaughn the Junkers. This was victory number five for Harley Vaughn, so the 82nd FG now had its sixth ace.

On the 23rd the 96th FS escorted some B-26s to Sardinia. Two single-engined Cant Z.501 flying boats were seen flying close to the surface of the water and both were shot down, one of them by Maj Vaughn.

The 95th flew another anti-shipping sweep on 28 April, but this time – as would henceforth often be the case – its P-38s' role was as both escort and bomber. The four Lightnings in one flight carried 500-lb bombs whilst the remaining 15 provided cover for both them and 18 Mitchells. Two Axis merchant ships were spotted, and the B-25s attacked one and the P-38 flight skip-bombed the other. 2Lt Richard F Kenney Jr, who was leading the second element in the fighter-bomber flight, scored a direct hit amidships. The shock wave from his bomb's explosion flipped his aircraft upside down, and as he righted it he saw some Bf 109s coming after him from above. Kenney turned into their attack and shot one of them down.

Meanwhile, Capt McArthur led the escort into some Bf 109s and C.202s and downed one of the former. Amongst the other claimants were 2Lts Bob Muir (a C.202) and James R Gant (a 'two-place, radial-engined Italian fighter'). Gant was flying Will Hattendorf's P-38F-15 *My Baby* (43-2181/'AY'). The results of this mission were six enemy aircraft and a ship destroyed. Muir's victim was evidently Sottotenente Vincenzo Graffeo of the *Regia Aeronautica's* 151° *Gruppo*, 367ª *Squadriglia*, who was killed after reportedly shooting down one of the two P-38s that were lost.

Shortly after noon on 29 April the 95th flew another sea sweep, to Cap Bon. This time 12 of its P-38s carried bombs whilst 14 others provided cover. Unfortunately, seven of them had to turn back because of mechanical problems and another crashed into the sea en route. Having nearly bombed a hospital ship by mistake, the P-38s were then attacked head-on by a large formation of Bf 109s. In the ensuing fight six German aircraft were claimed as shot down, with three more as

probables and one damaged, against the loss of two more Lightnings. II./JG 27 claimed three P-38s, two of them being credited to its *Kommandeur*, Hauptman Werner Schröer, as his 64th and 65th of an eventual 114 victories. Capt McArthur had downed one of the Bf 109s, this being his fifth kill to give the 82nd FG yet another ace. The biggest scorer was 2Lt Louis E Curdes (who was flying one of the fighter-bombers) with three confirmed and a damaged. Curdes, who had joined the 95th FS three weeks earlier, reported;

'After the bomb run, I was flying in a vic with Capt McArthur, and another flight of P-38s was right behind us. Capt McArthur suddenly called "Look out for the '109s!" and we banked sharply and pulled up in a steep turn to the right. A '109 came across my sights at a 45-degree angle, passing to the left. I kicked left rudder and followed it down. When within 300 yards and at about 30 degree deflection I let go a very long burst. I could see my tracers curving right into his nose. I broke off at 100 yards and passed in front of the '109, which nosed over and went straight in. There was a big splash and an oval of white foam.

'I straight-and-levelled and started to look for my wingman. A '109 came in from the right at a steep angle. I did a level turn tight to the right and the '109 went over me. I followed him down, shot several bursts and thought I saw pieces fall off. However, the '109 screamed off for home along the deck. I then turned around looking for company. Beneath me, I saw a P-38 100 ft above the deck on one engine. Three '109s were coming out from shore after him at heights of between 500 and 1000 ft and still one-and-a-half miles or so away. I started to head them off, climbing very slightly. They evidently didn't see me, and I gave the right-hand plane a big burst. This '109 was lagging a bit behind the other two, which were in a very tight formation. My tracers went into him, puffs of black and white smoke came out and he did a wingover straight in.

'The other '109s started to dive at the one-engined P-38. I made a 30-degree deflection shot at the leader, closing to 20 degrees and making about 350 mph. The '109 burst into flames, exploded and flopped into the water. I overshot both him and the P-38, lined up on the deck, and made a tight turnaround. The other '109 was pouring lead into the P-38. I came around on his tail, shot one burst, missed, and the '109 headed away for home. The other P-38 went into the sea.'

A few minutes later Curdes spotted some more Lightnings, one of which also ditched into the sea. Another, which was on a single engine, he led back to the coast. Shortly after crossing it they both were about to run out of fuel, so Lt Curdes landed wheels-down in a dry river bed whilst his companion belly-landed in a nearby field. The other pilot was picked up on 3 May and Curdes flew his aeroplane out on the 4th after gasoline and a few hundred feet of pierced steel planking (PSP) had been brought to the site.

Also on 3 May, a terrible tragedy struck the 95th FS. Capt McArthur was leading the unit on a B-26 escort/sea sweep when the weather closed in, forcing the P-38 pilots to turn back after they lost sight of the bombers. Most of them made it to Berteaux, although with considerable difficulty – when they landed the cloud base was at just 200 ft. McArthur and two other pilots in his flight landed at Bône,

This 95th FS P-38G-5 (42-12832/'AD') with very colourful nose art is believed to have been assigned to Lt Lou Curdes shortly after he shot down three Bf 109s and damaged another on 29 April 1943 (*Author*)

Ernie 'Hawk' Osher poses with his famous mount *"THE SAD SACK"* and its groundcrew after scoring his fifth victory with the fighter on 11 May. These men are, from left to right, TSgt Leroy Lee (crew chief), Sgt Bill Coy (assistant crew chief), Cpl Sorvando Velarde (armourer) and Capt Osher. When this photograph was taken *"THE SAD SACK"* had flown 'only' 86 of its eventual total of 183 combat missions (*USAF*)

in Algeria, but after taking off from there for home late that afternoon all three of them crashed into a mountain and were killed. Two more pilots from the 95th suffered the same fate that day. McArthur was succeeded as squadron CO by Ernie Osher.

The group's next air action came two days later when four flights from the 95th FS escorted some B-25s on another anti-shipping strike. The unit was led by Capt Osher in *"THE SAD SACK"* (his assigned aircraft), this being his first mission as CO. Over the Egadi Islands they encountered six SM.82 transports escorted by 16 C.202s (misidentified by the American pilots as 'Me 109s' and 'MC.200s'). Osher led two flights in to attack the enemy aircraft after first ordering the remaining two to stay with the Mitchells. In the ensuing action all the transports and three of the fighters were claimed destroyed and another fighter was damaged. Osher was credited with downing an 'MC.200' and one of the transports, whilst 2Lt Richard Kenney destroyed two SM.82s and a supposed 'Me 109'. These gave both men a total of four confirmed victories. Italian-American P-38 pilot 2Lt Guido F Lucini also downed an 'Me 109' and one of the SM.82s. Two of the 95th's pilots were killed by the Macchis, however.

One of the more unusual incidents in the annals of the 82nd FG took place on 6 May during a B-25 escort by the 96th FS. The formation was just north of Cap Serrat when 'Ricky' Zubarik's right engine began acting up and he turned back. However, it soon seemingly returned to normal, so the aggressive young lieutenant decided to reverse course again and rejoin his squadron.

Zubarik was flying east parallel to the shore about ten miles out to sea when five Me 210s appeared from the direction of the coast, headed towards him. Zubarik was at about 300 ft and the twin-engined Messerschmitts were just above the water. They opened fire when within range and he headed farther out to sea to escape them. The Messerschmitts turned to follow him, and he saw two of his pursuers collide and fall into the sea.

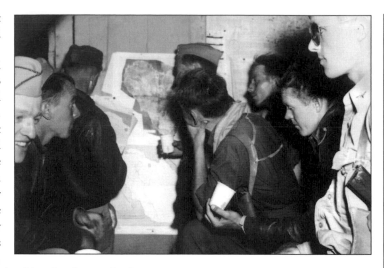

Nevertheless, the others stayed on Zubarik's tail and seemed to be gaining on him, despite his P-38 pulling 65 inches of mercury and indicating 350 mph. He then dropped his combat (Fowler) flaps and began a gradual climbing turn to the left. Zubarik started to gain on the Me 210s and finally got well above them. He then turned, dove on them and fired a short burst, before climbing away and heading for home.

Both of Zubarik's engines began to run away about 50 miles from Berteaux and he landed in a field. Tinkering with them for the rest of that day and most of the next, he finally got his P-38 back into the air on the evening of the 6th and flew the fighter home. Since he had no friendly witnesses to the Me 210s' demise, 'Ricky' was unable to obtain official credit for the two aeroplanes he had destroyed without firing a shot.

With little to contribute to the soon-to-be-concluded Tunisian campaign, the 95th and 96th FSs returned to Sicily on 11 May, escorting three groups of medium bombers over the harbour at Marsala. Bf 109s from II./JG 27 intervened, one of which was claimed destroyed by Capt Osher and *"THE SAD SACK"*. Another Messerschmitt and an Fw 190 were damaged. This kill made 'Hawk' Osher the 82nd FG's eighth ace.

Two days later USAAF bombers targeted Cagliari, on Sardinia, and when enemy fighters rose to engage them both the 96th and 97th FSs intervened. Lt Zubarik destroyed a C.200, thus giving him (officially) a total of five victories and, more importantly, ace status. The only other claim was made by Herman Visscher of the 97th, whose Bf 109 kill was his third victory.

13 May 1943 was also the day the remaining Axis forces in Tunisia finally surrendered to the Allies.

Despite being latecomers to North Africa, pilots of the 82nd FG had been credited with destroying more enemy aircraft (196) than any other USAAF fighter group in-theatre.

96th FS pilots attend a typically informal mission briefing at Berteaux in May 1943. On the far left is Lt 'Ricky' Zubarik and at the far right is Lt Samuel A 'Sammy' Hawes, who scored two victories. Next to Hawes (holding the cup) is Lt Herman 'Lee' Solem, whose final score was three destroyed, one probable and four damaged in the air, plus one enemy aircraft destroyed on the ground (*Author*)

Lt 'Ricky' Zubarik sits on the windscreen of his *Pearl III* (P-38G-10 42-13054/'BS'), camera in hand, right after becoming an ace on 13 May 1943 – as indicated by the five swastikas. He scored his sixth victory on the 21st, three days before he was shot down over Sardinia and made a PoW. The question marks are for the two Me 410s that collided while chasing him and *Pearl III* on 6 May, for which he received no official credit (*Crow*)

MEDITERRANEAN ISLES

Now that the Axis forces in North Africa had surrendered, the Allies' main goal in the Mediterranean was the invasion of Italy. But before that could take place four months hence, there were some strategic, Axis-held, islands – primarily Sardinia and Sicily – that would have to be neutralised first. They would now be the 82nd FG's primary targets.

The group's first post-surrender mission was the very next day, 14 May. It was a combination B-25 escort and dive-bombing assignment to Sardinia by the 95th and 96th FSs that was vigorously opposed by both flak and fighters, resulting in the loss of three P-38s. This was also the number of enemy aeroplanes claimed by the group in return. One of the latter was Bill Schildt's sixth, and final, kill (a 'single-engined Italian seaplane') in his P-38G-15 43-2406/'AX' *CAT SASS*. Maj Vaughn and 2Lt Lawrence P Liebers of the 96th were each credited with a C.202 destroyed. These were Liebers' first kill and Vaughn's seventh, and last.

Larry Liebers had been one of the group's original staff sergeant pilots prior to being transferred to the 78th FG in California. He went to England with the 78th at the end of 1942, but he and most of the group's other junior officers were sent to North Africa as P-38 replacement pilots several months later, and Liebers ended up back with the 82nd.

The group's next air battle over Sardinia was fought during the afternoon of the 19th, when the 95th FS escorted some B-25s to Villacidro. As the formation withdrew after bombing its target, eight Bf 109s commenced a running attack that continued far out to sea, where they were joined by other Axis fighters. The P-38 pilots were subsequently credited with five Bf 109s destroyed, three probables and two damaged. A lone C.200 was also destroyed. Lt Lou Curdes was credited with downing two of the Messerschmitts, giving him a total of five kills in just two missions since joining the squadron in mid-April. The 82nd had another ace! Lt Danny Sharp also claimed a Bf 109 for his fourth confirmed victory. No Lightnings were lost.

'Blackie' Oliver (on the left), Lou Curdes (in the centre) and Ralph C Embrey (right) all scored confirmed Bf 109 kills over Sardinia on the 95th FS's 19 May 1943 mission – one, two and one, respectively. His victories that day made Lt Curdes an ace. This was Lt Oliver's only kill, whilst Lt Embrey, who flew a second P-38 combat tour with the 474th FG in Europe, finished the war with two victories to his name (*USAF*)

Curdes was interviewed by a reporter about this mission;

'As we left Villacidro I was wingman to Lt Kenney. My leader chased one ME 109 off the tail of the first element and another came in at about a 30-degree angle. I shot him down. We were attacked again and everyone seemed mixed up. In the middle of the fight I had to switch gas tanks. Then, as Kenney's guns were jammed, we hit the deck for home at about 400 mph. But these MEs were fast and persistent and three dived at us from the rear, about 30 miles south of Sardinia. Having my guns working, I took the lead and Kenney followed me into a right turn into them. I fired at the first ME and missed, but he took off. The second one I shot into the sea and Kenney bluffed the third one away.'

If his guns had not jammed Richard Kenney would almost certainly have scored his fifth kill in this fight. Sixty-nine years later, he still regrets his missed opportunity to become an ace;

'I was on the tail of the third '109, but was a tiger with no claws. He didn't know I had no guns and broke away, headed for home. I often thought over the years that I could have cut his tail off with my left engine!'

The 97th FS took off 15 minutes after the 95th to escort some more B-25s to another airfield in Sardinia. There was little aerial opposition left by the time they arrived – just a Bf 109 and two Italian fighters that made a single pass at the P-38s after the bombing as the formation was heading for home. 1Lt Herman Visscher shot down the Messerschmitt for his fourth confirmed victory. Later that month he was reassigned temporarily to the Fighter Replacement Training Center as a P-38 instructor.

The following day it was the 96th's turn to accompany the Mitchells to Villacidro, where a mixture of German and Italian single-engined fighters and several Ju 88s were encountered. 1Lt 'Dixie' Sloan shot down one of the Junkers and a C.200 and damaged two Bf 109s, Flt Off Frank

These 96th FS pilots had all just scored confirmed victories over Villacidro, Sardinia, on 20 May 1943. They are, from left to right, 2Lt Ward Kuentzel, 2Lt Ed Waters, 1Lt 'Dixie' Sloan, 1Lt Marvin R Jones, Flt Off Frank Hurlbut and 1Lt P D Rodgers. The Bf 109 that Jones shot down that day was his only aerial claim (*USAF*)

Hurlbut downed an Fw 190 and damaged a Bf 109, 1Lt Wayne Jorda destroyed a Bf 109 and probably destroyed a C.200, 2nd Lts Ward Kuentzel and Ed Waters each destroyed one of the Messerschmitts and 1Lt P D Rodgers shot down a C.202. There were no American losses against credits totalling eight destroyed, one probable and three damaged.

The group returned to Sardinia for the third day in a row on the 21st, and once again met aggressive, persistent – and futile – opposition. First off was the 96th FS, escorting B-25s to Villacidro. Up to 20 Bf 109s and C.202s met them in the target area, and 2Lt Larry Liebers shot down one of the Italian fighters. Engaging the Bf 109s, 2Lt Paul Cochran destroyed one (his fifth victory, making him an ace) and 1Lt 'Ricky' Zubarik another (his sixth), bringing the squadron's total to four destroyed and one damaged. The 97th was right behind them, shepherding more Mitchells to the same target. It too met and engaged about 20 enemy fighters, its pilots claiming three destroyed, including an Fw 190 downed by 1Lt Gerry Rounds, and four probables. Once again there were no losses to the 82nd FG.

The first mission on 24 May was yet another B-25 escort, to a landing ground near Olbia, on Sardinia, by the 96th FS in the early afternoon. As they approached the target clouds of dust were visible below – enemy fighters taking off. The P-38 pilots formed a Lufbery Circle before being attacked by some C.202s. By the time the Italian pilots gave up the fight, two of their aeroplanes had been shot down, one probably destroyed and six damaged. The confirmed victories were by 2Lts Clarence Johnson and 'Lee' Solem. Johnson, who preferred to be called either by his initials, C O, or 'Tuffy', was one of the replacement pilots who had joined the 96th the previous month.

This time there was a single, particularly unfortunate, loss, as Lt Zubarik was last seen leaving the 'Lufbery'. After returning from the mission, his close friend 'Dixie' Sloan took off again in a refuelled and rearmed P-38 on an unauthorised solo search mission. On a deserted Sardinian beach he spotted the burning wreckage of his buddy's aeroplane, but there was no sign of its pilot. He finally gave up and went home, assuming 'Ricky' was dead – and was greeted with considerable official displeasure when he arrived back at Berteaux. Three months later word was received that Zubarik was in fact a PoW.

The 97th FS followed the 96th to Sardinia 20 minutes later, four of its flights escorting B-26s whilst the remaining three, led by Gerry Rounds, went in ahead of the Marauders and dive-bombed the target. A few Axis fighters intervened, without success, and several of them were shot down. The squadron's claims for three

Harley Vaughn and Larry Liebers in a typical North African scene. Lt Liebers has just scored the second of his eventual seven victories (a C.202 over Sardinia on 21 May), whilst Maj Vaughn had claimed his seventh, and last, one week earlier (*USAF*)

destroyed, one probable and one damaged included a Bf 109 destroyed by Lt Rounds after his 500-lb bomb had hit a hangar on Alghero airfield.

SOUK-EL-ARBA

In early June the 82nd FG began its next move, to Souk-el-Arba in western Tunisia. The RAF, which had previously occupied the airfield, had named it 'Marylebone' after an affluent area of London. The 82nd's personnel were fully installed there by the middle of the month. Meanwhile, on 12 June, a 96th FS pilot became the group's first to complete a 50-mission combat tour.

One of the 95th FS's best pilots was lost on 15 June as he strafed a radar station in Sicily. 2Lt Richard Kenney was hit by flak and crash-landed near the target to spend the rest of the war as a PoW. Later that day the 97th also flew to Sicily as escorts for a formation of B-25s, which was attacked by enemy fighters. A C.202 was destroyed by 1Lt Ray Crawford for his sixth, and final, victory, a Bf 109 was probably destroyed and another Messerschmitt fighter was damaged.

The 96th FS flew a particularly successful mission on the 18th – an escort of 310th BG Mitchells to Aranci Gulf, Sardinia. The bombers were intercepted by an estimated 50 enemy fighters, the first small group of which had appeared 20 miles south of the target. The P-38s immediately went into a 'Lufbery'. Many more Axis machines had

An informal debriefing takes place at Berteaux following a mission by the 96th FS in late May 1943. At bottom left, Capt Daniel 'Mac' MacDonald, the squadron's intelligence officer, makes notes on the fender of a vehicle while the pilots enjoy coffee and donuts that were dispensed from the Red Cross truck in the background. This group includes four of the squadron's aces – Larry Liebers (on the far right, holding a cup of coffee), Frank Hurlbut (facing him, eating a donut), 'Dixie' Sloan (at upper left, with his hand over his mouth) and 'Shorty' Waters (wearing the cap and sunglasses) (USAF)

entered the fray by the time the B-25s reached Aranci, and enemy pilots continued to make attacking passes until the bombers were well on their way home. The 96th subsequently claimed 16 Axis fighters destroyed, two probables and eight damaged for the loss of just one of its own. The top scorer was Larry Liebers, who was credited with two C.202s and a Macchi C.205 destroyed and two more C.202s damaged. These gave him a total of five confirmed kills (all of them Macchi fighters) and made him the group's 12th ace. Frank Hurlbut claimed a Bf 109 and a Reggiane Re.2001 fighter destroyed and another Messerschmitt as a probable, whilst 'Dixie' Sloan claimed a C.200 destroyed (his eighth victory) and another damaged.

'Shorty' Waters scored his third kill in this fight;

'As we neared the target I saw an Me 109 making a head-on attack from our left. Six of us turned towards him and he immediately broke away. My wingman and I, being the closest, took out after him. He was in a left turn and I cut inside of him. My first burst hit his tail. The next burst hit directly in the cockpit. He straightened out and began to dive. We followed him down to 5000 ft, but his speed was so great that we couldn't keep up with him. He attempted to pull away but couldn't. The aeroplane completely disintegrated upon contact with the water.'

'Shorty' was not Lt Waters' only nickname, some of his squadronmates calling him 'Duck Butt'. This was, he recalled later, because he had been seen 'walking over to my aircraft with my parachute on, hanging below my knees, and waddling like a duck'.

The other victors that day included Ward Kuentzel (a C.202 destroyed for his third victory and two others damaged), Wayne Jorda (a probable

These were among the 13 96th FS pilots who scored a total of 16 confirmed victories over Sardinia on 18 June 1943. In the front row, from left to right, are 2Lt Ed Waters, 1Lt Larry Liebers and Flt Offs Frank Hurlbut and Walter J Mackey (who scored an Fw 190 for his only confirmed kill). In the back row, from left to right, are 2Lt Ward Kuentzel, 1Lt John Perrone, 2Lt George T Fitzgibbon (who downed a C.202 for his only aircraft claim), Flt Off John R Rawson (a C.202 destroyed that day, plus a probable C.202 on 24 May), 2Lt Louis E Pape (a confirmed C.202, plus a probable Fw 190 on 10 July), 2Lt Donald W Johnson (a C.202, plus another on 2 September) and unknown. The scores of the other pilots (all aces) are mentioned in the text. Unfortunately, the identity of *"SPUD's"* pilot (who, according to the scoreboard on its gondola, had at least four victories) is not known (*USAF*)

Fw 190), Fred Wolfe (a C.202 destroyed and a Bf 109 damaged) and John Perrone (a C.202 destroyed). This was Maj Vaughn's 50th, and last, mission, the 96th FS CO being sent home a week later. He subsequently saw further action late in the war as deputy CO of the 33rd FG in India and Burma, once again flying P-38s.

21 June was another notable day, as it saw the group's first, albeit rather uneventful, mission to Italy escorting B-25s to a rail junction near Naples. It also marked the first appearance of American fighters over the Italian mainland. This was mission No 50 for the 82nd's other two squadron commanders, Maj Osher of the 95th and the 97th's Capt 'Pete' Petersen, who received his promotion to major before he left.

The 95th FS flew another B-25 escort to Aranci Gulf on the 24th, during which Lou Curdes made the only claim, downing a C.202 for his sixth victory. Four days later the 95th and 96th were assigned a similar mission to Sardinia, the target this time being Alghero airfield. The 95th scored a probable whilst the 96th's pilots claimed two destroyed, one probable and two damaged (all C.202s). C O Johnson got his squadron's probable, and the confirmed kills went to Ward Kuentzel and Ed Waters, the latter becoming the group's latest ace with this claim.

The 82nd's last air combat in June came on the 30th, when the 96th FS accompanied B-25s to the airfield at Sciacca, in Sicily. The target was successfully bombed and enemy fighters did not put in an appearance until the formation was over the sea on its way home. During the ensuing fight the P-38 pilots claimed two Fw 190s and a Bf 109 destroyed and another Messerschmitt fighter damaged. Lt Waters downed one of the Focke-Wulfs for his sixth kill. This was mission No 50 for Wayne Jorda, making him the group's latest tour-expired pilot. He was also another 'almost an ace', having been credited with four destroyed, two probables and one damaged.

OPERATION *HUSKY*

The invasion of Sicily, codenamed Operation *Husky* and scheduled for 10 July, was now at hand. In addition to the bombers' 'softening-up' process, the fighters' job would be to establish air superiority – a prerequisite to any invasion. This was a task for which the 82nd FG's Lightning pilots were eminently qualified, as they soon demonstrated.

First off as part of the group's 4th of July 'celebration', at 1040 hrs, was the 97th FS on a B-25 escort to the airfield complex at Gerbini. Enemy fighters were encountered and three destroyed, one probably destroyed and seven damaged, against the loss of a P-38.

Two hours later the 95th flew an identical mission, and also ran into some aerial opposition over Gerbini. Its claims, all against C.202s, were for three destroyed, two probables and one damaged, without loss. 2Lts Jim Gant and Bob Muir each got a confirmed victory, whilst 2Lt Danny Sharp was credited with one of the probables. Sharp tried very hard – though unsuccessfully – to get it confirmed as destroyed, as he was about to complete his tour and had four kills to his name. This would have made him an ace, but it was not to be. Sharp flew his 50th mission six days later without adding to his score of four destroyed, three probables and one damaged – about as close as a fighter pilot can get to being an ace without actually attaining that coveted status.

Gerry Rounds' *CADIZ EAGLE* (whose serial number is unfortunately unknown) was photographed at Souk-el-Arba shortly after its pilot's fourth victory on 5 July 1943 (as per the four swastikas, plus the 12 bomb symbols indicating the aeroplane's bombing missions). The fighter would soon be renamed *Chicken Dit*. The two men are its crew chief, TSgt Calvert 'Willie' Wilson (on the left), and his assistant, Sgt Phillip Oswalt (*Wilson*)

97th FS ace Ray Crawford flew his 50th mission – another B-25 escort to Gerbini – late the following morning. An hour later the 96th and the rest of the 97th took off for an identical assignment. Unlike the previous mission, this time there was plenty of opposition, numerous enemy fighters attacking the American formation after the bombing. The Lightning pilots claimed five kills, including a Bf 109 and an Re.2001 by 'Dixie' Sloan and another Bf 109 by Gerry Rounds, without loss. These victories gave Lt Sloan a total of ten, tying him as the top-scoring USAAF pilot in the MTO with Maj Levi Chase, a squadron commander in the P-40 Warhawk-equipped 33rd FG.

From 8 through 11 July the air echelons of the 96th and 97th FSs operated from the RAF base at Misurata, on the coast of Libya. This placed the units closer to the Allied invasion convoys that they were to cover as the vessels sailed from Egypt to Sicily, whilst the 95th FS was sent to Monastir, on the Tunisian coast. Just before this move, two more 96th FS pilots completed their combat tours, John Perrone on the 6th and P D Rodgers the following day. Both men had four confirmed kills.

In the late afternoon of 10 July 24 Lightnings from the 96th FS were on a fighter sweep covering the Sicily landings when 16 enemy fighters – Fw 190s, Bf 109s and C.200s – were seen scrambling from the airfields at Castelvetrano and Carcitella. A Ju 88 that was also caught taking off was quickly shot down by Ward Kuentzel. The Fw 190s were from fighter-bomber unit *Schlachtgeschwader* (SG) 10, targeting the invasion fleet off Gela. By the time this air battle had ended, the 96th's pilots had accounted for no fewer than ten enemy aircraft destroyed, two probably destroyed and eight damaged, for one loss. Flt Off Frank Hurlbut claimed three Fw 190s destroyed and one damaged, while Lt Ward Kuentzel also downed a Focke-Wulf and damaged two more, in addition to his Ju 88. These victories took Kuentzel's tally to six kills and Hurlbut's to seven, thus making them both aces.

Hurlbut remembered that whilst circling the island 'formations of Focke-Wulfs began to take to the air from Palermo and other nearby airfields. They quickly rose to our altitude, and the fight began. The first Focke-Wulf was banking in front of me – it was very close, and I hardly had to use my gunsight. I set it on fire and saw it circle down to the left, but didn't see it crash. Other enemy fighters were all over the place and I turned my attention to them. Suddenly, a "Lufbery" developed, made up of Focke-Wulfs and P-38s in singles and doubles – all in single-file and swinging in a banking turn to the left, first climbing, then descending. It seemed like everyone was firing at the ships in front of them all at the same time.

'I was closing quickly on a single Fw 190 that was climbing, and again came up close behind and inside him. Behind me was another P-38 with a Focke-Wulf on his tail, and a P-38 on the Fw 190's tail. We were all

These 96th FS pilots all scored confirmed kills during a fighter sweep over Sicily on 10 July 1943. They are, from left to right, 'Dixie' Sloan, Frank Hurlbut, Ed Waters, Larry Liebers, Lincoln D 'Linc' Jones and Ward Kuentzel. The Fw 190 he shot down that day was Lt Jones' second, and last, victory (*USAF*)

playing follow-the-leader. I was very close to the Fw 190 in front of me and hit him with three quick bursts. He went over on one wing and then fell into a spin, before crashing in Sicily.

'I recall I was very concerned about the P-38 on my tail, who was following my manoeuvres and who was being pursued by the second Focke-Wulf. I would fire, then look back and yell over the radio for my friend to watch out for the enemy fighter on his tail. I was the luckiest, I guess, because the guy behind me was on my side. The other Nazi aeroplane in our game of crack-the-whip apparently was damaged, as he dropped out and left the area. Another Fw 190 cut across and in front of me from the right. I led him and fired, hitting him as he flew through my fire, but he kept on going and cut back to the right. I claimed him as a damaged.

'We then dived down looking for more of them, and I found my third whilst descending. I looked down and saw him skipping along close to the water, heading for Sicily. He had a P-38 chasing him some distance back, but he was pulling away and leaving the Lightning behind. I had plenty of speed, so I dove down between them and started to shoot. My first burst got him and he looped over and crashed into the sea.

'I claimed the two aeroplanes I had seen crash, but also got credit for the first one because other pilots in our squadron had seen it go down.'

Also enjoying success during the course of this mission were Larry Liebers (an Fw 190 destroyed and two damaged), 'Dixie' Sloan (a C.200

destroyed), Ed Waters (a Bf 109 destroyed) and Fred Wolfe (an Fw 190 destroyed). For Liebers this was victory number six, whilst Waters had claimed his seventh, and last. 'Shorty' would complete his tour six days later, as had his squadronmate and fellow ace 1Lt Paul Cochran on that day's first mission. Lt Wolfe completed his tour a few days later, with four kills. He subsequently served another P-38 combat tour with the 474th FG in Europe. Cochran was sent to the Pacific in 1945 to fly P-51s with the 21st FG on Iwo Jima, escorting Superfortresses to Japan. Unfortunately, before he could fly any such missions he was wounded during a Japanese suicide squad attack on Iwo Jima and ended up in a hospital, instead of in the cockpit of a Mustang over the Home Islands.

Flt Off Frank Hurlbut returned from the 10 July 1943 mission tired but happy, having scored three confirmed victories to become an ace (*Hurlbut*)

Lt Sloan's victory gave him a total of 11 kills, making him the top USAAF ace in the MTO. He described this success many years later;

'All of a sudden I'm on the tail of a P-38 and he's firing away at an MC.200. I watched with admiration until suddenly he broke away. I thought, "Why did he pull away? The Macchi looks OK to me". I moved in on it and was just about to fire when its canopy flew off and the pilot bailed out. I almost hit him with my wing. I can still remember coming so close I could see the buttons on his flight suit.'

On 17 July Bill Schildt led the 95th FS on a B-25 escort to Naples, which was his 50th, and last, mission. He too would later serve in the Pacific, but in his case as an Air Transport Command pilot flying four-engined C-54 transports.

The 96th FS returned to Italy with the Mitchells on the 22nd, their target being the railway junction at Battopaglia. Enemy fighters were encountered shortly after the bombing, when three Bf 109s came at the formation from below, near the coast. They were quickly driven off, however, Ward Kuentzel damaging one of them in the process. Two other Bf 109s dove on the B-25s just beyond the shoreline, but they were

This publicity shot of six 82nd FG aces was taken in mid-July 1943. They are, from left to right, Ward Kuentzel (96th FS), Frank Hurlbut (96th), Ray Crawford (97th), Larry Liebers (96th), 'Dixie' Sloan (96th) and Lou Curdes (95th) (*USAF*)

intercepted by Kuentzel and 'Dixie' Sloan. The two P-38 pilots came so close to the enemy aircraft that they could see their yellow spinners and bellies and bright green camouflage paint. They could even make out the heads of the Messerschmitts' pilots in their yellow helmets. They fired simultaneously and both German aeroplanes erupted in flames and fell into the sea.

Lt Sloan, who would finish his tour five days later, now had 12 confirmed victories to his name. He retained his status as the top USAAF ace in the Mediterranean Theatre of Operations for another eight months until Maj Herschel

Bill Schildt was photographed with his last Lightning (P-38G-15 43-2406) around the time he completed his combat tour on 17 July 1943 (*Schildt*)

'Dixie' Sloan poses with his faithful P-38G-5 42-12835/'BO' *Snooks IV½* shortly before returning to the USA in early August 1943. He scored the last of the 12 victories displayed on its nose, a Bf 109, over Italy on 22 July (*Stanaway*)

'Herky' Green, a P-40 and P-47 pilot with the 325th FG, scored his 13th kill in March 1944. The only other P-38 pilot in the Mediterranean or Europe to match Sloan's score was 1Lt Michael Brezas of the 14th FG, who claimed his 12th, and final, aerial victory in August 1944.

There was an interesting postscript to 'Dixie' Sloan's story. He remembered that when he went home he was told to stop in Algiers and report to Lt Gen Carl 'Tooey' Spaatz, Commander of the Twelfth Air Force. 'They didn't tell me why, but he was going to pin the Distinguished Flying Cross on me. When his adjutant read the citation, the general stopped the ceremony to have the thing rewritten for the Distinguished Service Cross [DSC]. The adjutant went back and did that. Spaatz signed the citation and gave it to me, telling me that he would send the medal to my commander back home. I never got it'. In 1968, by which time Sloan was a retired lieutenant colonel, his son contacted the also retired Gen Spaatz and asked him to have this oversight corrected. The general was happy to do so, and in February 1969 he personally awarded 'Dixie' the Air Force Cross in lieu

The 96th's Lt Ward Kuentzel discusses the operation of his P-38's four 0.50-cal machine guns with his armourer, Cpl Howard Shaffner (*USAF*)

These 96th FS pilots all completed their tours in July 1943 and had been sent home by the end of that month, with a total of 29 confirmed victories between them. They are, from left to right, Lts Paul Cochran (5), John Perrone (4), Ed Waters (7), Lincoln Jones (2), P D Rodgers (4), Fred Wolfe (4) and Bernard L 'Bull' Barber (3). 'Linc' Jones was just 19 years old at this time (*John Stanaway*)

of his long overdue DSC, which is second only to the Medal of Honor. It had been awarded to him for his heroism on 5 July 1943.

A B-25 escort to the airfield at Pratica di Mare, in Italy, on 30 July was Ward Kuentzel's 50th mission. He had been selected to fly one of the group's veteran P-38s across the Atlantic to the USA so it could be featured on a War Bond tour. Unfortunately, one of its engines caught fire over the ocean shortly after he left Casablanca and Kuentzel had to bail out near a British destroyer, which quickly picked him up. He subsequently returned home via more conventional transport. Kuentzel joined a new fighter group, the 479th, in the USA and travelled with it to England, and the Eighth Air Force, in May 1944. On 19 June, whilst flying at high altitude over France on a bomber escort mission, Capt Kuentzel's oxygen system failed, as a result of which he lost consciousness and crashed to his death in P-38J-15 42-104427.

GROMBALIA

It was also on 30 July that the 82nd began moving to its new base at Grombalia, near Cap Bon in Tunisia. This move, which was completed by 4 August, would place the group closer to its targets in Sicily and Italy.

With the success of the Sicilian campaign by now a foregone conclusion, the 82nd FG's missions alternated between supporting it and attacking strategic targets on the Italian mainland. On the afternoon of 7 August the 96th FS was assigned to escort four B-25Gs (each of which carried a huge 75 mm cannon in its nose) targeting enemy shipping in the Gulf of Eufemia between Pizzo and Palmi, in Italy. Eight of its Lightnings carried bombs. Low clouds impeded both the fighters and the fighter-bombers, although the Mitchells did find some targets in Pizzo harbour.

At this point four enemy fighters – two Fw 190s and two Bf 109s – came down out of the cloud cover and attacked the bomb-carrying P-38s, whose pilots dropped their loads and turned into them. Flt Off Frank Hurlbut and 2Lt Don Warr each hit an Fw 190 and they both crashed into the sea below, but not before one of them had fatally damaged the P-38 flown by the No 3 man in their flight, 2Lt Richard Drayton, who was killed. Hurlbut also damaged one of the Messerschmitts. His quick reactions were admirable, especially considering that he had just been released from hospital and was still recovering from a 'full-blown case of malaria', which had left him 'very weak and somewhat out of it'.

The official end of the Sicilian campaign came on the 17th, when Allied forces entered Messina, on the island's east coast. Amongst the pilots who completed their tours at this time was the 95th FS's Lt Will Hattendorf. Plans had been made for Hattendorf to fly his aeroplane, *My Baby*, home as Ward Kuentzel had attempted to do with another P-38 a couple of weeks earlier, but at the last minute he was ordered to return to the USA by ship instead.

Frank Hurlbut's P-38G-10 42-13174 *Hell's Angel* was loaded with a 500-lb bomb and a drop tank for the 7 August 1943 mission that saw him shoot down an Fw 190 for his eighth confirmed kill (*Hurlbut*)

ITALY – TARGET AND HOME

Whilst accompanying some B-25s to Benevento, in Italy, on 20 August 1943, the 96th and 97th FSs engaged the enemy in the air once again. Shortly after the formation crossed the Italian coast en route to the target at around 1330 hrs, ten Bf 109s dove on it from out of the sun and shot down a straggling 97th pilot. During the withdrawal 15 more enemy fighters jumped the Lightnings. The 96th's 2Lt C O Johnson was ready for them this time, and he quickly turned in behind a flight of Fw 190s, shooting one of them down and damaging another. He then got on the tail of a third and lost several thousand feet as he manoeuvred for a shot. He finally fired, and hit its pilot just as he climbed out of the cockpit. Johnson's squadronmate 2Lt Larry Liebers was also credited with an Fw 190 for his seventh, and last, victory (he completed his tour eight days later). However, two more Lightning pilots were posted missing in action after this mission, the total claims for which were four destroyed and two damaged.

2Lt Larry Liebers chats with his crew chief, TSgt Roswell Harding, on the wing of his P-38 whilst assistant crew chief Sgt Leroy Garman and armourer Cpl Wendell Stoltz work on it. Liebers shot down an Fw 190 near Benevento, in Italy, on 20 August 1943 for his seventh, and last, victory. He completed his tour at the end of that month (*USAF*)

The mission to which the group was assigned on 25 August was different from any it had flown before. The 82nd, together with the 1st FG and part of the 14th FG, was ordered to execute a low-level attack on the large complex of enemy airfields in the plains surrounding the city of Foggia in east central Italy. Its purpose was to destroy, by strafing, as many enemy aircraft on the ground as possible, thus reducing the number that would be available to oppose the Italy invasion forces. Leading the mission was Lt Col George M MacNicol, the 82nd FG's new deputy CO, who had previously served in the South Pacific.

Takeoff began at 0630 hrs. The 82nd was joined over the Gulf of Tunis by the 1st and 14th FGs, creating an aerial armada comprised of more than 150 P-38s. At an altitude of less than 100 ft, and maintaining strict radio silence, they flew over Sicily, headed northeast across the Italian Peninsula and then flew north along the Gulf of Manfredonia to just below the city of the same name, where the Lightnings turned southwest toward Foggia, approximately 20 miles away. When they neared that city the individual squadrons and flights proceeded to their assigned airfields. As they approached them at more than 300 mph and just 20 ft above the ground, it quickly became apparent that they had achieved nearly complete surprise.

Lt Col MacNicol, at the head of the 97th, led most of that squadron and the 96th over Foggia Satellite Airfield No 7, where he destroyed an Fw 190. Five other aircraft were also claimed destroyed there on the ground, including a C.202 by 2Lt Sammy E McGuffin of the 97th and a Ju 52/3m by the 96th's 1Lt 'Lee' Solem. The latter's aeroplane was badly damaged by anti-aircraft fire, however, and he wondered for a while if he was going to make it home. Solem did not that day, but he did make it to the group's refuelling and emergency stop in Sicily, where he spent the night. Coincidentally, this was Solem's 50th, and last, combat mission. He went home shortly thereafter with a score of three destroyed, one probable and four damaged in the air and the Ju 52/3m as his solitary strafing victory.

Just three 96th FS pilots and one from the 97th attacked airfield No 9. The only confirmed kills there were all claimed by Flt Off Urban F Stahl of the latter unit, who exploded and/or burned four Ju 88s. The 95th was the most successful squadron, destroying 11 aeroplanes on airfield No 3, including a Ju 88, a Bf 109 and a Ju 52/3m credited to Lt Guido Lucini, who had two previous aerial victories. Having destroyed a C.202 on the ground, 1Lt Tom Hodgson then encountered some enemy aircraft in the air;

'I was leading a flight of four aeroplanes. We came in low at Satellite No 3, ducking under a high tension wire just before we hit the field. I found a Macchi 202 Italian fighter ahead of me on the ground and gave it a spurt. It went up in flames. The other boys got several ships. Then we were over the far edge of the field, so we broke up the line abreast formation and bunched together in a little group, with me leading the way. I looked around to check the other three ships, and at that instant I saw two of them hit the ground. For a moment I thought it must be flak, and then, as I watched, the third ship went in too, and I could feel shots hitting my own aeroplane. Then I saw two Italian Macchi 202 fighters that had trailed us across the field. I was the only one left of my flight. I gave my ship hard

Lou Curdes and his second assigned Lightning, probably P-38G-10 42-13150/'AZ', in which he was shot down on 27 August 1943 to become a PoW (Author)

left rudder and turned into them, but they got away. Then, because I was pretty well banged up myself, I hit the deck and beat it home.'

A 96th FS pilot was also missing in action. The 82nd had claimed 21 enemy aircraft destroyed on the ground, plus several dozen more and considerable other enemy materiel damaged (the 1st and 14th FGs claimed a further 50 aircraft destroyed between them). Shortly after the strafing the Foggia airfields were bombed by B-17s escorted by the rest of the 14th FG, resulting in the destruction of an additional 47 Axis aircraft.

Immediately upon their return to Grombalia, Lt Col MacNicol was personally awarded a DFC for his leadership of the mission by Lt Gen Spaatz. Later, the 82nd FG received its first Distinguished Unit Citation (DUC) for the part the group played in the mission, as did the 1st FG. The following day MacNicol assumed command of the group, and a week later Maj William P Litton, a West Point graduate who had previously flown P-39s in the Aleutians, became his deputy.

The 82nd lost one of its aces to enemy action on the morning of 27 August during another B-25 escort to Benevento by the 95th FS. Fifty enemy fighters met the USAAF formation over the coast near Naples and a swirling dogfight ensued, during which 2Lt Lou Curdes became separated from the rest of his flight whilst damaging a Bf 109. This did not deter him, however, and he continued to fight until he had shot down another Messerschmitt. Curdes then saw a P-38 in trouble, went to its aid and downed another Bf 109, thus increasing his score to eight destroyed and two damaged – the best the remaining 95th pilots could do was two damaged.

However, Curdes lost his squadronmate to enemy fighters and one of his engines took some serious hits before he finally headed for home. He seemed to have the situation under control as he reached the Italian coast, but his other engine was then damaged by a burst of flak. Curdes knew his Lightning (P-38G-10 42-13150/'AZ') was done for, so he crash-landed it on a beach a few miles south of Salerno, set it on fire and awaited his inevitable capture.

Lt Curdes and some other PoWs escaped from their Italian jail on the morning of 4 September, but they were recaptured almost immediately and sent to a maximum security camp. Four days later the Italian government agreed to an armistice with the Allies, whereupon the PoWs were given rifles and blankets by their former guards and then allowed to walk away. Unfortunately, the ex-PoWs were far behind the German lines, and for the next eight months they lived as fugitives, aided by Italian partisans. Curdes finally crossed into Allied-controlled territory on 27 May 1944, exactly nine months after he had been reported missing in action. After returning home he soon volunteered for another combat tour, this time in the Philippines, flying P-51s with the 3rd Air Commando Group. During this tour Curdes claimed a single Japanese aircraft destroyed.

The early afternoon of 28 August brought another B-25 raid on the Naples area, with the bombers escorted by the 96th and 97th FSs on this occasion. Enemy aircraft were encountered once again, resulting in claims for three destroyed and two damaged, all by the 97th. Two of the kills were scored by 1Lt Herman Visscher and Flt Off Urban Stahl. Visscher's was significant, as it gave him a total of five, making him the group's 16th ace. He had returned from his temporary training assignment earlier that month, and finally completed his combat tour on 8 September. Stahl had finished his tour three days earlier, having been credited with one aerial victory and four strafing kills. Unfortunately, just as he was about to begin another tour in the Pacific, Stahl was killed in a flying accident in P-38J-20 44-23357 in Hawaii on 1 December 1944.

SEE NAPLES AND DIE

As exciting as the 82nd FG's 25 August DUC mission had been, the one to which it was assigned eight days later made this pale by comparison. Some 74 P-38s were to accompany 72 B-25s to the marshalling yard at Cancello, near Naples, in what on paper appeared to be a typical medium bomber escort. However, the mission turned out to be anything but typical. 96th FS pilot Fred A Selle remembered years later that pilots within the group had adopted the popular pre-war travel slogan 'See Naples and Die' to describe these missions. For the one on 2 September 1943, this turned out to be eerily prophetic.

There was no interference prior to the bomb run. The Mitchells hit the target and then, as they dropped their noses to pick up speed in the dash for the Italian coast, 15 to 20 particularly aggressive enemy fighters – a mixture of Bf 109s and C.202s – plummeted down on them. The 96th FS intervened to protect the bombers, commencing a savage dogfight as the rest of the formation escaped to the southwest. More of the enemy then entered the fray and the 96th's pilots were quickly overwhelmed and forced to call for help, whereupon several flights from the 95th FS turned back to assist them.

By the time they crossed the coast the B-25s were far ahead and clear of the fighting. The participating P-38 pilots then tried to break free of the melée but their opponents were persistent. Lt Selle had heard a warning call ('Timber!') and then several Bf 109s came down onto the rear of his flight. He recalled that he got his 'tanks off and cockpit under control, and was still in formation as we rolled out of the turn'. Selle quickly damaged two of the Messerschmitts, whilst at the same time trying to avoid the hostile attentions of numerous others. 'After another warning of attack', he went into a tight spiral to pick up speed and lost his wingman. Another P-38 tucked in on his right wing just in time to turn with him to meet a Bf 109 head-on. Selle fired a short burst and noted strikes on the enemy's propeller and wingroot. The Messerschmitt then rolled to its left and collided with Selle's new wingman, both pilots bailing out of their stricken aircraft.

Thirty Axis fighters continued to attack the 96th FS just north of the island of Ischia at about 2000 ft, forcing the P-38 pilots to dive for the wave tops so as to protect the bellies of their aircraft. When they finally reached the deck, the Lightning

All of Lt Fred Selle's aerial claims (for three Bf 109s destroyed and two damaged) resulted from the 2 September 1943 B-25 escort to Naples. The 96th FS pilot also destroyed an enemy aircraft on the ground later that month. He is pictured here (left) with a pilot of the Allied Italian Co-Belligerent Air Force at Lecce, in Italy, in November (*Selle*)

pilots realised that they were still outnumbered, and now at a tactical disadvantage. They once again made calls for help, which were answered by more pilots from the other two squadrons.

Fred Selle had by then turned back several times to assist other P-38s, and his fuel was now reaching a critical level due to him having utilised full power for such a long time. He and two others, now just above the water, bored through the mass of milling fighters to make a run for home. Selle looked up and saw another Bf 109 coming straight for him at a slightly higher altitude. He pulled up the nose of his P-38, fired a burst into the Messerschmitt's engine and belly and was stunned to see it explode in flames right in front of him.

The force of the explosion flung Selle's Lightning onto its back, leaving him upside down and heading in the wrong direction, just 20 ft above the water! After he had regained control of his aeroplane and cleared his tail, Selle took a 15-degree deflection shot at another Bf 109, which spun into the water from 200 ft. He then spotted yet another enemy fighter, which was on the tail of a Lightning. Selle fired a burst from 100 yards and closed to within 25 yards before he ran out of ammunition. This Bf 109 also broke up and crashed in flames. Lt Selle was credited with three confirmed kills and two damaged.

More than 100 fighters were now battling it out at low altitude over the sea, many of them in large defensive circles, with numerous splashes in the water below indicating shot-down aircraft. Also in the middle of the action was Selle's squadronmate Frank Hurlbut (in his P-38G-10 42-13174 *Hell's Angel*), who remembered;

'We had fought our way down to the water so that they couldn't hit us from below – only from the sides or from above. This gave us a little less to worry about. Two Me 109s in line astern dove down right next to me, then pulled up and away to the right. I broke into them as they came down, only to find that I had been suckered away from my flight, which had continued to the left, just above the water. Immediately thereafter, two other '109s attacked me from above. They were flying line abreast and came in to close range. I could see their guns flashing as I looked back and up through my canopy. At the same time two more Me 109s, flying close together, were closing in from approximately 90 degrees directly above my canopy, firing as they came.

'I was in a maximum performance turn to the left and an extreme cross-controlled skid to the right. This was a trick I had learned that I used in combat many times. When enemy fighters were trying to hit me I would bank violently whilst cross-controlling, standing on the inside rudder and racking the aircraft into a turn. This caused the aeroplane to slide sideways and fly erratically in a somewhat different flight path from the direction it *appeared* to be going in. This technique probably saved my life once again, because even though all four enemy aircraft were right on top of me, and the water just below was churning from cannon and machine gun fire, they all completely missed me – thank God!

'As I was getting back with the other P-38s in the area, another single Me 109 was down at my level. The pilot was banking around to the right and cutting directly in front of me. I straightened out my aircraft for a few seconds, led him with my guns and started firing. He flew right through my line of fire and then simply peeled over and went into the sea. I wasn't sure whether he had gone in because of my fire or had simply forgotten in the heat of battle what his altitude was when he peeled away.'

This was Flt Off Hurlbut's ninth, and last, aerial victory. He completed his combat tour four days later.

Amongst the other successful 96th FS pilots were 2Lt Leslie E 'Andy' Andersen (two Bf 109s destroyed and another damaged), 2Lt C O Johnson (one Bf 109 destroyed and two probably destroyed) and 1Lt Bill Vantrease (one Bf 109 destroyed and one probably destroyed, giving him his final total of three destroyed and one probable). 1Lt Tom Hodgson of the 95th, who was flying his 50th mission, downed an Re.2001, whilst his squadronmate 2Lt Jim Gant claimed two C.202s, giving him a total of four kills. In the 97th, 2Lt Robert B Williams Jr was credited with two Bf 109s destroyed. Gant, Johnson and Vantrease would all finish their tours in the next two weeks.

The credits for this mission totalled 23 destroyed, five probables and eight damaged, but this success had come at a terrible cost. Ten of the group's pilots were missing in action, and it was later determined that eight had been killed and two had survived as PoWs. Their sacrifice was not in vain, however, as not a single B-25 was lost. For its pilots' valour that day, the 82nd FG received its second DUC.

Amongst the various Axis units the group fought on 2 September was III./JG 53, whose 8. *Staffel Kommandeur*, Oberleutnant Franz Schiess (an *experte* with 67 victories), was killed in this action. He had been credited with shooting down 16 P-38s in the Mediterranean since December, including some from the 82nd FG.

Lt Leslie 'Andy' Andersen (on the right), who joined the 96th FS in June 1943, scored his first two kills, plus a probable, on the 2 September DUC mission. In this photograph he is posing with his squadronmates Lt Dana Lovejoy (on the left) and Capt Bradley Prann at Lecce two months later. He scored two more victories on 6 December and another four days later to achieve ace status. Unfortunately, no photograph could be located of Andersen's assigned aircraft, P-38G-10 42-13026/'BV' *Pugnacious Peggy*, which was later transferred to the Fifteenth Air Force's 154th Weather Reconnaissance Squadron (*Fred Selle*)

SALERNO

The initial Allied landings on the Italian mainland took place the following day when British troops went ashore at Reggio di Calabria, on the 'toe' of the Italian 'boot'. To cover the upcoming American landings at Salerno, just south of Naples (codenamed Operation *Avalanche*), the 82nd FG's air echelons moved temporarily to Maddelina – Gerbini Satellite Airfield No 2 – on Sicily. The move began on 5 September and was completed two days later. And it was on the 5th, whilst still flying from Grombalia, that the 82nd next scored in the air when Lt Bob Muir of the 95th FS shot down a C.202 during a B-25 escort to Grazzanise.

The group began covering the invasion fleets on 8 September (the day the Italian government capitulated) and then the Salerno landings on the 9th. Its first interception of enemy aircraft near the beachhead took place on the afternoon of the 11th, when Bf 109s of I. and II./JG 53 flew a *freie Jagd* (fighter sweep) to Salerno. The Luftwaffe pilots spotted the P-38s of the 97th FS and attacked them. Despite being outnumbered, the Lightning pilots claimed five Bf 109s destroyed and two damaged. One of the victors was squadron operations officer Gerry Rounds, whose kill took his tally to five, making him the 82nd FG's 17th ace. He later described what happened;

'The controller vectored us towards what they called "eight bogies". Upon arriving at the spot where the controller said the bogies were, we saw 12 aeroplanes in a typical P-40 formation – flights of four, with all aeroplanes in line abreast. We met them slightly staggered, as they were a little off to our right. Just before reaching the abreast point, they turned into us. At the same time, 12 more came down from the rear, making it a perfectly coordinated attack. With our eight aeroplanes against their 24, the situation looked a little one-sided, with us on the losing end.

'After the initial attack, we formed a "Lufbery" in two directions. That is, we were meeting aeroplanes of our own outfit head-on, in vertical banks. We had to stay and fight, but we weren't worrying about it because we had full gas tanks – more than they had. Our belly tanks, used whilst on patrol, were dropped the minute we started to attack.

'The '109s would dive down at us in pairs, but as soon as they got within range there was always a P-38 meeting them head-on. No matter how they came in, someone was always in position to level out, fire a burst and get back in the circle. The German pilots dropped off one by one, and after about ten minutes, when they had lost five, they decided that they had had enough and started for home.'

This engagement was not all one-sided, however, as Rounds' P-38, *Chicken Dit* ('CD'), received some vital hits, one of which knocked out its hydraulic system. The fighter was virtually destroyed in its subsequent belly-landing in Sicily. Lt Rounds flew ten more missions before the end of September, setting an 82nd FG record of 82. His many decorations included a Silver Star.

Scoring his first confirmed aerial victory in this fight was 2Lt Sammy McGuffin, who lost an engine in the process but still made it back to Maddelina. The following day McGuffin probably destroyed an Fw 190 when more than a dozen enemy fighters were encountered by the 97th near the beachhead (a Bf 109 was also probably destroyed).

The group's last mission from Sicily, on 18 September, was another strafing attack on various Foggia airfields. Its P-38s took off from Maddelina early that morning and later returned to Grombalia. Sixteen Axis aircraft were claimed destroyed this time and many more were damaged. Lt Col MacNicol led this one, too, once again at the head of the 97th FS, and he was credited with destroying two unidentified single-engined fighters. His deputy, Maj Bill Litton, who was flying with the 96th, destroyed another, as did squadron pilot Lt Selle. 95th FS CO Capt Hugh M Muse Jr claimed a Ju 88. Three of the P-38s were lost to flak, however.

Gerry Rounds had very mixed emotions when this unfortunately poor quality photograph was taken at Gerbini, on Sicily, on 11 September 1943. He had just scored his fifth victory – a Bf 109 over the Salerno beachhead – but had to crash-land his beloved *Chicken Dit* because of the damage it received in that fight (*Rounds*)

These two shots of Lt Will Hattendorf's *My Baby* (P-38F-15 43-2181/'AY') were taken around the time he completed his combat tour in August. The photo below shows Hattendorf and his crew chief, Sgt Vern Taylor, next to the right side of its nose, displaying the five victory markings and the painting of Will's 'Baby' (wife), Betty. The left side, shown in the photo to right, also displays the symbols representing the aeroplane's 11 bombing missions. The identity of the officer posing in front of the P-38 is not known. The 96th FS's Lt C O Johnson flew this aeroplane back to the USA for a War Bond drive on 26 September 1943 (*Hattendorf*)

Fred Selle completed his tour at the end of November, having claimed three aerial victories and one strafing success. He served another tour in the Pacific in 1945, flying P-47s from Okinawa.

Most of the tour-expired pilots who went home around this time had volunteered to fly a few extra missions during the Salerno beachhead crisis. Amongst them was the 96th FS's 1Lt C O Johnson, who flew his 50th on 14 September, but volunteered for four more before departing on the 26th. His transport home was not the norm, as he flew Will Hattendorf's P-38F-15 *My Baby* (43-2181/'AY') back to the USA for a War Bond tour. Johnson would see a lot more action before his war's premature end. Assigned (along with his former squadronmate Ward Kuentzel) to new P-38 group the 479th whilst it was still in America, he went with it to England in May 1944. Johnson subsequently scored the 479th FG's first aerial victory (his fifth) and then transferred to fellow Eighth Air Force outfit the 352nd FG, which was equipped with the P-51. Promoted to captain, Johnson had scored two more aerial kills and six strafing victories by the time he fell victim to an Fw 190 on 23 September 1944.

The 82nd FG flew its last mission from Grombalia – and from North Africa – on 30 September 1943. It was moving time again.

ON TO ITALY

Most of the group's ground echelon moved to its temporary new home – San Pancrazio/Salentina, a former *Regia Aeronautica* base on the heel of the Italian 'boot' – on 2 October, followed the next day by its pilots. As it turned out, the 82nd's stay at San Pancrazio would last only a week, during which time it flew just eight missions.

The group was now within range of the Axis-controlled Balkan countries, and in the coming weeks its pilots would be frequent visitors to Greece and Yugoslavia, in particular. On 6 October the 82nd was assigned to strafe the airfield in the Greek town of Araxos, the 96th FS providing cover as the 95th and 97th attacked various targets. The mission was led by Lt Col MacNicol at the head of the latter squadron, and he destroyed an unidentified single-engined fighter and damaged an Fw 190. Amongst the other aircraft destroyed – all by pilots from the 97th – was an unidentified single-engined fighter claimed by 2Lt Bob Williams. The group tally was seven destroyed and seven damaged.

The pilots saw their next air action on 8 October during a B-25 escort to Athens' Eleusis airfield by the 95th and 96th FSs. As they left the target after the Mitchells had dropped their ordnance, 12 Bf 109s from JG 27 attacked the 95th from above and behind, thereby commencing a running fight over the Gulf of Corinth that resulted in two confirmed kills and four damaged for the loss of two P-38s. One of the downed Messerschmitts was victory number four for 2Lt Bob Muir, who completed his tour the following week.

On the afternoon of the 9th the 97th FS escorted four B-25Gs on a sweep over the Adriatic Sea. A lone Ju 88 was spotted and shot up by all four members of one flight before it crashed. As the 82nd did not award shared victories, the pilots in such cases had to come to a mutual agreement as to who received the official credit, often by flipping a coin. In this case 'lots' were cast and the winner was Bob Williams.

The group moved again the following day, but it did not have far to go – just 20 miles east to San Donato airfield, near Lecce (this subsequently became the USAAF's name for the base), which would be its home for the next three months. Also known as Aeroporto Galatina, it was, like San Pancrazio, a pre-war base with concrete runways.

14 October brought another B-25 escort, this time to Argos airfield in Greece. Eight Bf 109s from III./JG 27 were spotted near the target and Maj Muse led his 95th FS flight in a bounce on four of them. Muse destroyed one and probably downed another, but a P-38 in turn fell to the enemy fighters.

On the 20th the group flew a combination B-25 escort and dive-bombing mission to the marshalling yard at Nis, in Yugoslavia. A lot of damage was done there, and a nearby airfield was strafed as well, resulting in claims for three enemy aircraft destroyed and eight damaged. The former included an SM.82 transport credited to Lt Col MacNicol, who this time was flying with the 96th FS.

Two days later the 82nd returned to Eleusis with the Mitchells. As the formation was departing the target area after the bombing, it was jumped by 20 enemy fighters. A 96th FS flight closed with some Bf 109s, one of which was shot down, whilst a second was probably destroyed by 2Lt Hiram C Pitts. Another Bf 109 was destroyed by 2Lt Paul F Jorgensen of the 97th and three Fw 190s were claimed as damaged.

A strafing mission was flown to the airfield at Tirana, in Albania, on 23 October. The 97th FS provided cover as the 95th FS attacked, the latter unit claiming four aircraft destroyed and five damaged. One of the 95th's flight leaders, 1Lt Claud E Ford, caught a Ju 52/3m in the landing pattern and shot it down. 'Hank' Ford had been one of the squadron's original staff sergeant pilots back in the USA, but he had transferred out due to illness before it went overseas and was subsequently assigned stateside P-38 instruction duty. He had rejoined the 82nd FG in August.

1Lt Clarence 'C O' Johnson on leave in the USA between combat tours, having flown Will Hattendorf's *My Baby* across the Atlantic from North Africa. Oddly, the emblem on his A-2 jacket's patch (the Slugging Desert Jack Rabbit?) seems to have been intentionally obscured. His score with the 96th FS was four victories, three probables and one damaged – oh so close to being an ace. However, Johnson made up for that failure by scoring three more kills in the air, plus six on the ground, while serving with the 479th and 352nd FGs of the Eighth Air Force in England. Then-Capt Johnson was killed in action with the 352nd (while flying a P-51) on 23 September 1944 (*Author*)

COLOUR PLATES

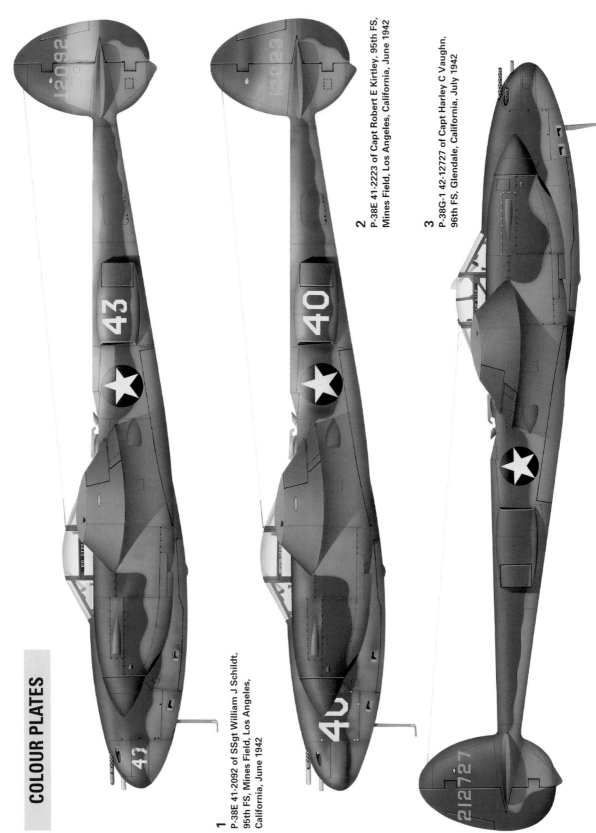

1
P-38E 41-2092 of SSgt William J Schildt, 95th FS, Mines Field, Los Angeles, California, June 1942

2
P-38E 41-2223 of Capt Robert E Kirtley, 95th FS, Mines Field, Los Angeles, California, June 1942

3
P-38G-1 42-12727 of Capt Harley C Vaughn, 96th FS, Glendale, California, July 1942

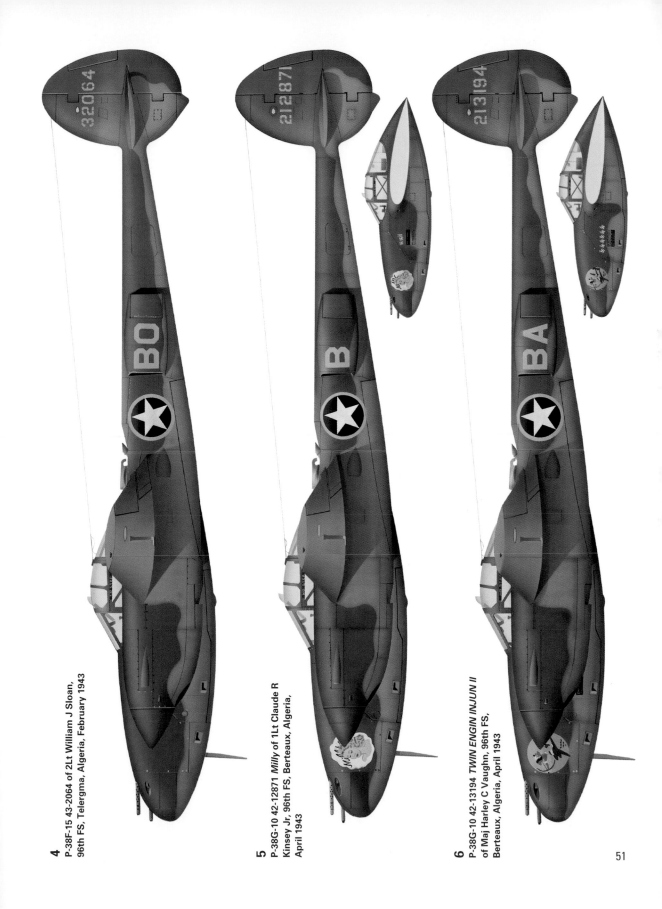

4
P-38F-15 43-2064 of 2Lt William J Sloan,
96th FS, Telergma, Algeria, February 1943

5
P-38G-10 42-12871 *Milly* of 1Lt Claude R
Kinsey Jr, 96th FS, Berteaux, Algeria,
April 1943

6
P-38G-10 42-13194 *TWIN ENGIN INJUN II*
of Maj Harley C Vaughn, 96th FS,
Berteaux, Algeria, April 1943

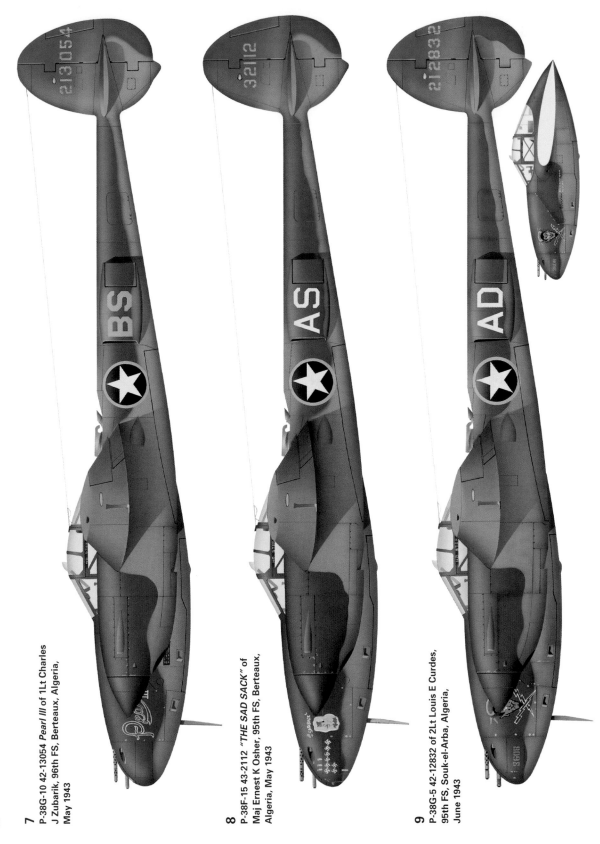

7
P-38G-10 42-13054 *Pearl III* of 1Lt Charles
J Zubarik, 96th FS, Berteaux, Algeria,
May 1943

8
P-38F-15 43-2112 *"THE SAD SACK"* of
Maj Ernest K Osher, 95th FS, Berteaux,
Algeria, May 1943

9
P-38G-5 42-12832 of 2Lt Louis E Curdes,
95th FS, Souk-el-Arba, Algeria,
June 1943

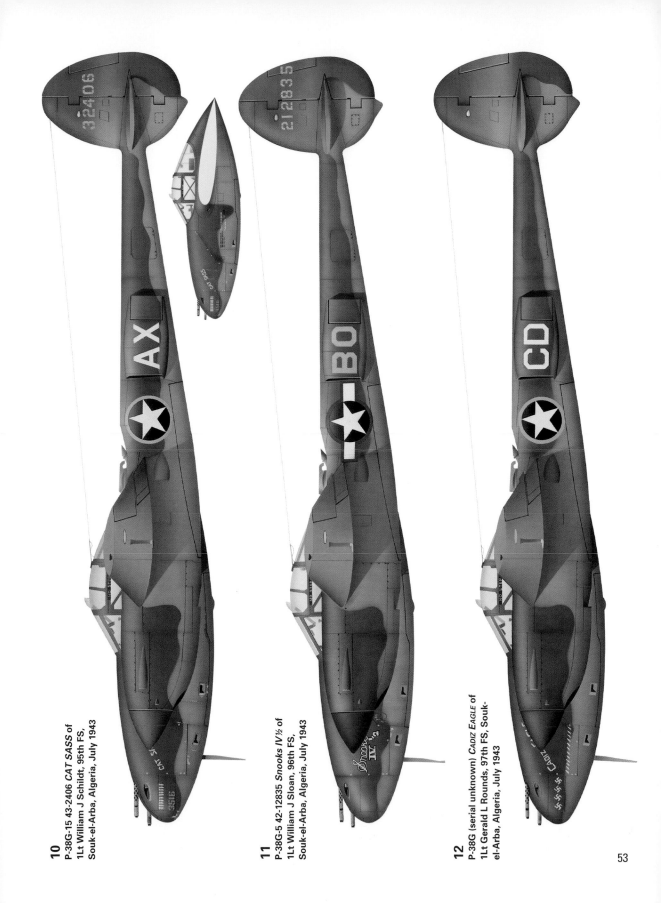

10
P-38G-15 43-2406 *CAT SASS* of
1Lt William J Schildt, 95th FS,
Souk-el-Arba, Algeria, July 1943

11
P-38G-5 42-12835 *Snooks IV½* of
1Lt William J Sloan, 96th FS,
Souk-el-Arba, Algeria, July 1943

12
P-38G (serial unknown) *CADIZ EAGLE* of
1Lt Gerald L Rounds, 97th FS, Souk-
el-Arba, Algeria, July 1943

53

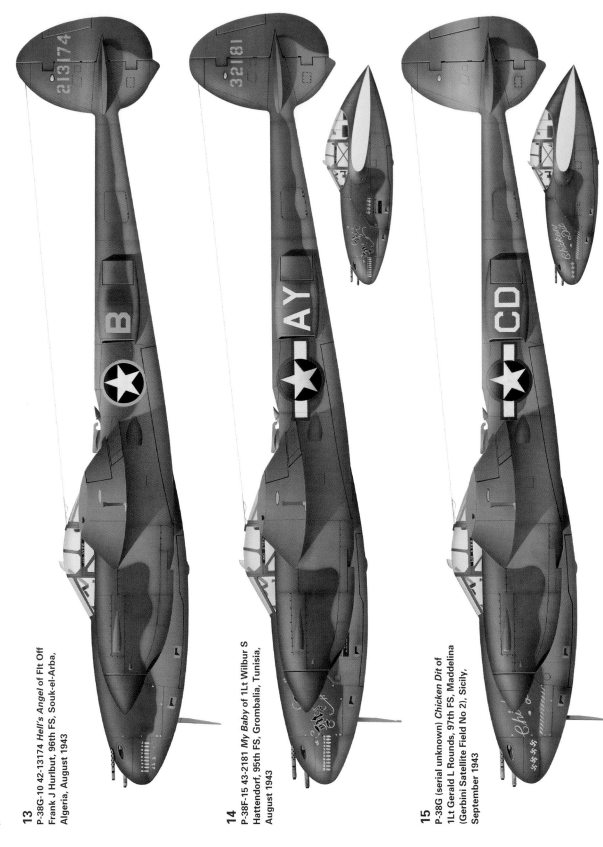

13
P-38G-10 42-13174 *Hell's Angel* of Flt Off
Frank J Hurlbut, 96th FS, Souk-el-Arba,
Algeria, August 1943

14
P-38F-15 43-2181 *My Baby* of 1Lt Wilbur S
Hattendorf, 95th FS, Grombalia, Tunisia,
August 1943

15
P-38G (serial unknown) *Chicken Dit* of
1Lt Gerald L Rounds, 97th FS, Maddelina
(Gerbini Satellite Field No 2), Sicily,
September 1943

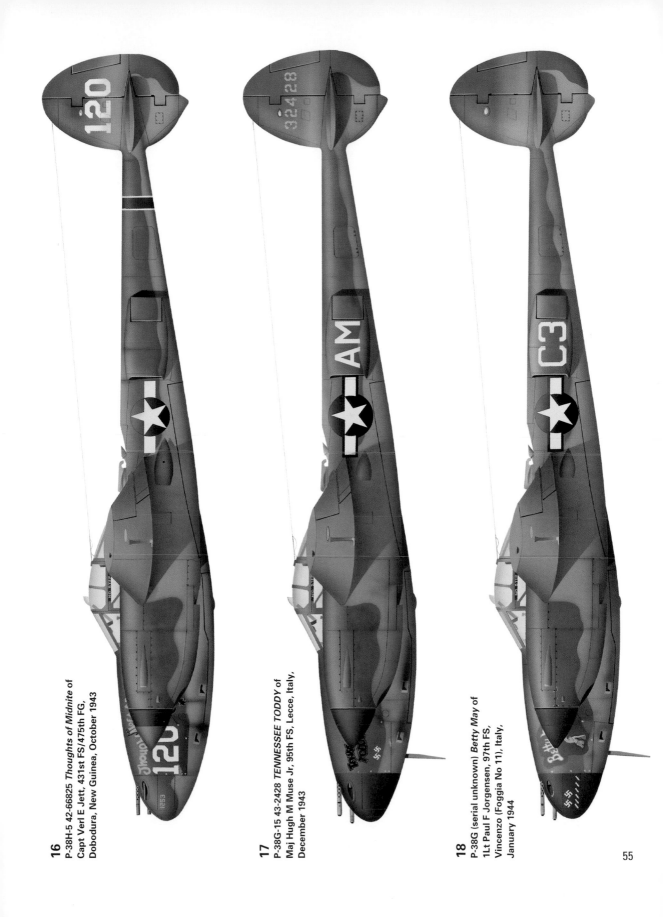

16
P-38H-5 42-66825 *Thoughts of Midnite* of
Capt Verl E Jett, 431st FS/475th FG,
Dobodura, New Guinea, October 1943

17
P-38G-15 43-2428 *TENNESSEE TODDY* of
Maj Hugh M Muse Jr, 95th FS, Lecce, Italy,
December 1943

18
P-38G (serial unknown) *Betty May* of
1Lt Paul F Jorgensen, 97th FS,
Vincenzo (Foggia No 11), Italy,
January 1944

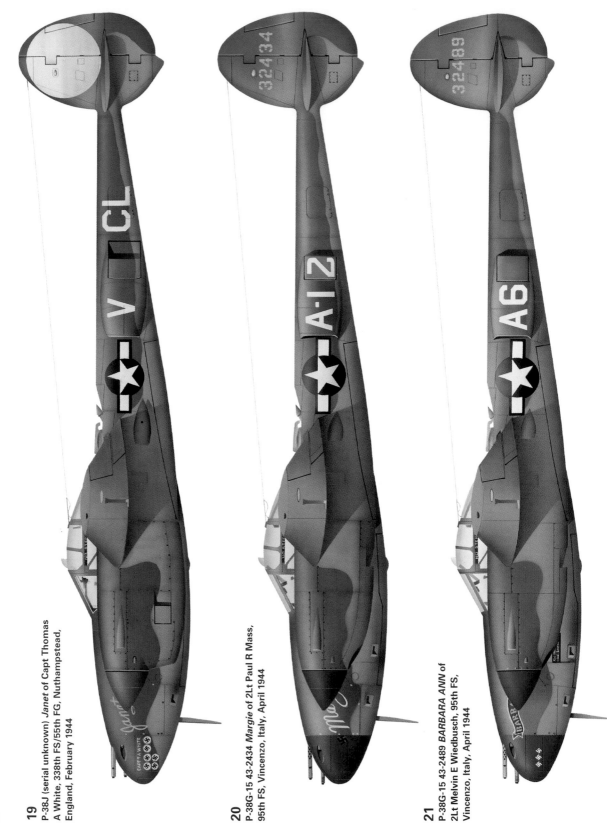

19
P-38J (serial unknown) *Janet* of Capt Thomas
A White, 338th FS/55th FG, Nuthampstead,
England, February 1944

20
P-38G-15 43-2434 *Margie* of 2Lt Paul R Mass,
95th FS, Vincenzo, Italy, April 1944

21
P-38G-15 43-2489 *BARBARA ANN* of
2Lt Melvin E Wiedbusch, 95th FS,
Vincenzo, Italy, April 1944

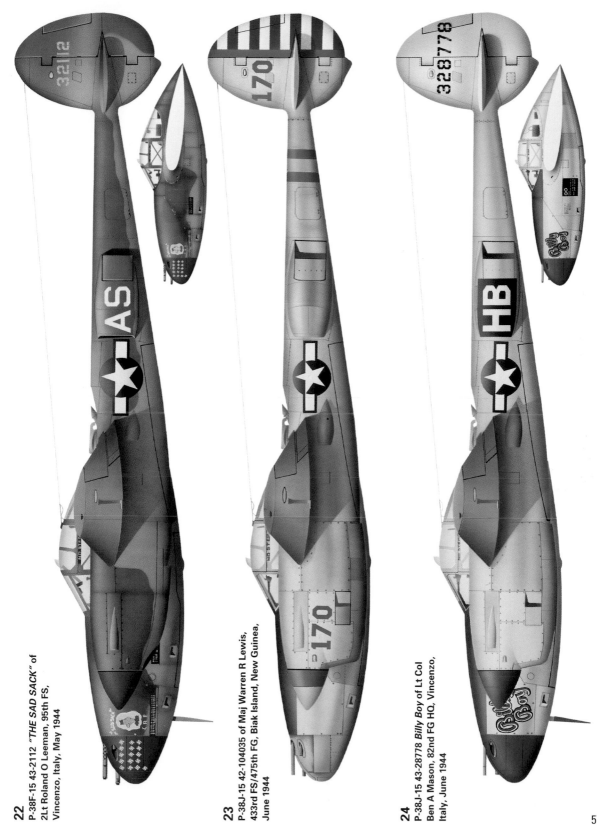

22
P-38F-15 43-2112 *"THE SAD SACK"* of
2Lt Roland O Leeman, 95th FS,
Vincenzo, Italy, May 1944

23
P-38J-15 42-104035 of Maj Warren R Lewis,
433rd FS/475th FG, Biak Island, New Guinea,
June 1944

24
P-38J-15 43-28778 *Billy Boy* of Lt Col
Ben A Mason, 82nd FG HQ, Vincenzo,
Italy, June 1944

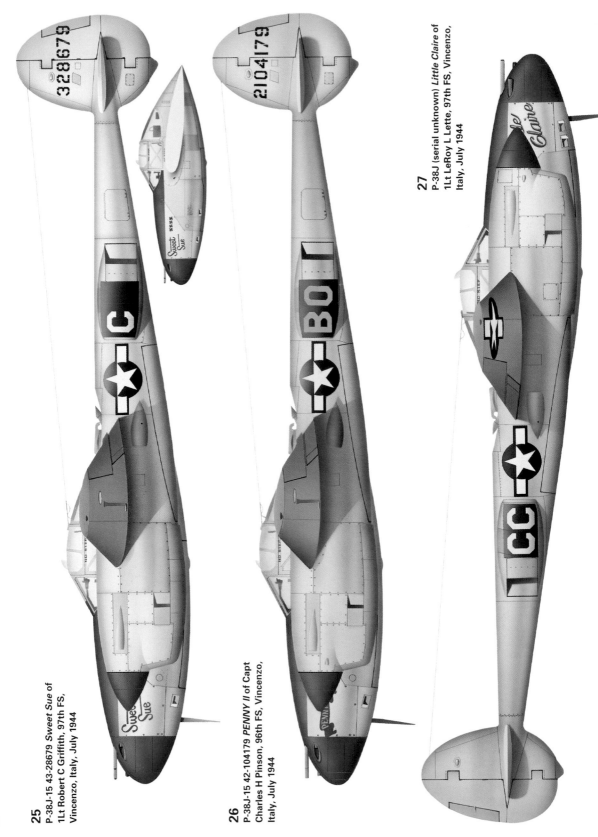

25
P-38J-15 43-28679 *Sweet Sue* of
1Lt Robert C Griffith, 97th FS,
Vincenzo, Italy, July 1944

26
P-38J-15 42-104179 *PENNY II* of Capt
Charles H Pinson, 96th FS, Vincenzo,
Italy, July 1944

27
P-38J (serial unknown) *Little Claire* of
1Lt LeRoy L Lette, 97th FS, Vincenzo,
Italy, July 1944

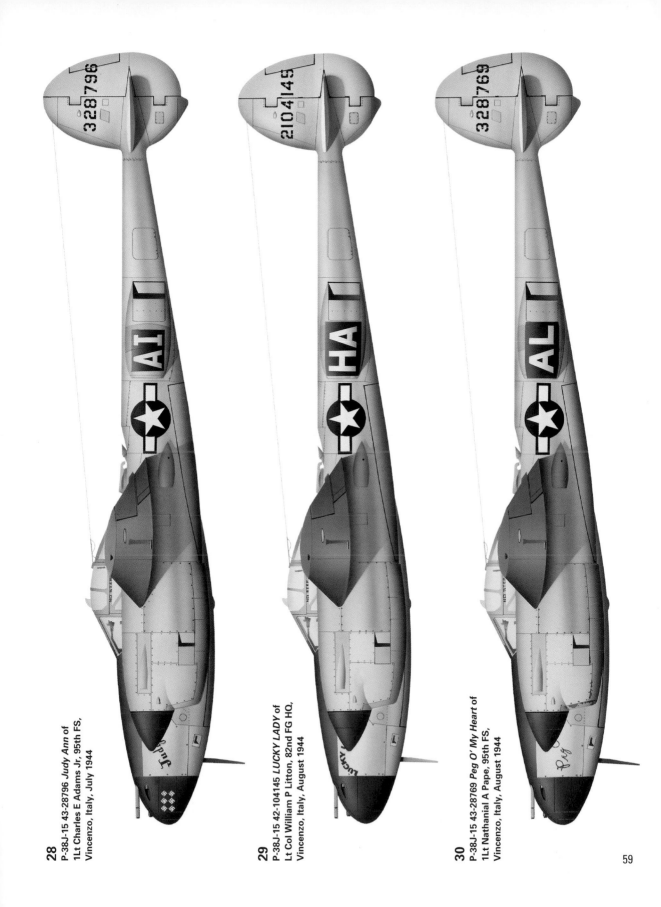

28
P-38J-15 43-28796 *Judy Ann* of
1Lt Charles E Adams Jr, 95th FS,
Vincenzo, Italy, July 1944

29
P-38J-15 42-104145 *LUCKY LADY* of
Lt Col William P Litton, 82nd FG HQ,
Vincenzo, Italy, August 1944

30
P-38J-15 43-28769 *Peg O' My Heart* of
1Lt Nathanial A Pape, 95th FS,
Vincenzo, Italy, August 1944

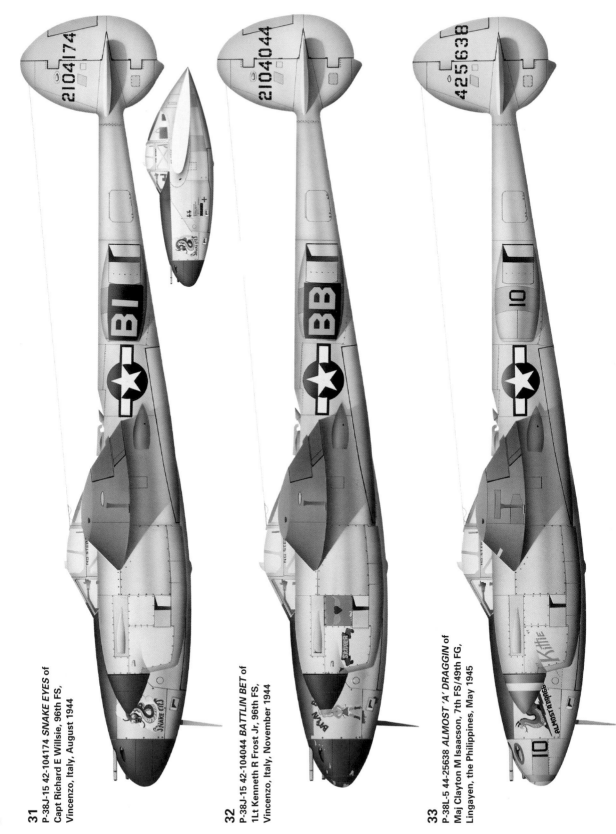

31
P-38J-15 42-104174 *SNAKE EYES* of
Capt Richard E Willsie, 96th FS,
Vincenzo, Italy, August 1944

32
P-38J-15 42-104044 *BATTLIN BET* of
1Lt Kenneth R Frost Jr, 96th FS,
Vincenzo, Italy, November 1944

33
P-38L-5 44-25638 *ALMOST 'A' DRAGGIN* of
Maj Clayton M Isaacson, 7th FS/49th FG,
Lingayen, the Philippines, May 1945

34
P-38J-25 (serial unknown) of 1Lt Lawrence
P Liebers, 429th FS/474th FG, Langensalza,
Germany, June 1945

Right
This photograph of the group scoreboard, taken at Vincenzo, in Italy, in 1945, displays what was then considered to be the 82nd FG's official total of confirmed aerial victories as of VE Day – 550. In fact, two turned out *not* to be confirmed, so the actual total was 548. The board also shows 176 enemy aircraft destroyed on the ground, plus nine ships sunk and 126 locomotives destroyed. Next to the pilots' names are their individual scores of enemy aircraft destroyed in the air (indicated by swastikas and fasces symbols), plus ship symbols indicating those credited with sinking same. Note the squadron emblems just below the evocative *KRAUT EXTERMINATORS INC.* title (*Author*)

61

STRATEGIC LIGHTNINGS

24 October 1943 was a notable date in the history of the 82nd FG. It marked the group's first high-altitude, long-range strategic bomber escort mission – the type that would predominate for the next year-and-a-half. Some 48 Lightnings took off from Lecce that morning, their task being to accompany Twelfth Air Force B-17 Flying Fortresses and B-24 Liberators – whose target was Wiener Neustadt, in Austria – as far as Lake Balaton, in Hungary. Despite its historical significance, the mission was rather uneventful as far as the 82nd FG was concerned.

The group's assignment the following day was more familiar, and successful. It was a strafe attack by the 97th FS on the airfield at Podgorica, in Yugoslavia, led by Maj Litton from Group HQ. Three enemy aircraft were destroyed on the ground – including an unidentified tri-motor by Litton and a Bf 109 by Lt Charles W Hicks – and seven more damaged. As the squadron withdrew it was attacked by three enemy fighters, one of which was damaged. Shortly thereafter, as the pilots neared the Albanian coast, 2Lt Bob Williams (in P-38G-13 43-2354) disappeared and was never seen again. He had been credited with three confirmed kills in the air and one on the ground prior to his demise.

The 82nd FG flew its last missions, and scored its final victories, as part of the Twelfth Air Force on 31 October. The claims were all made by the 97th FS, which strafed the airfield at Tirana. An Fi 156 liaison aircraft was shot down en route and the P-38s were attacked on the way home by some Bf 109s, three of which were also claimed destroyed (one of them by Capt John S Litchfield). No enemy aircraft were claimed destroyed on the airfield, however. Litchfield was one of the group's original staff sergeant pilots who transferred out in California, only to rejoin it overseas in the autumn of 1943.

A new strategic air force – the Fifteenth – was activated in Italy on 1 November under the command of Maj Gen 'Jimmie' Doolittle. It was comprised initially of the Twelfth Air Force's six heavy bomber groups, plus its three P-38 groups and one P-47 group for escort duty. The Twelfth would now be strictly a tactical air force.

The 82nd FG's first really productive mission with the Fifteenth Air Force came on 14 November when it escorted B-25s to Sofia, in Bulgaria – the first USAAF raid on that Axis country. Enemy fighters contested this incursion, resulting in claims totalling five destroyed, one probable and three damaged. Amongst the aircraft shot down were single Bf 109s for Capt Charles R Spencer and 2Lt Sammy McGuffin of the 97th FS, while the probable was claimed by their squadronmate 1Lt Jack Walker, who had recently returned from his temporary assignment with the *Armée de l'Air*. Three days later the 82nd escorted the Mitchells to

Jack Walker returned to the 97th FS from his training duties in October 1943. Coincidentally, his remaining aerial claims resulted from combats during bomber escort missions to Sofia, in Bulgaria. They included a Bf 109 probably destroyed and one damaged on 14 November, another probable Bf 109 ten days later, a confirmed Fw 190 on 10 December and a Bf 109 destroyed on 24 January, giving him an official total of four destroyed, three probably destroyed and one damaged. Walker's Lightning, *Elaine II* (serial number unknown), was named after his fiancée back in California, whom he married after returning home in March. The seven swastikas either included his probables or they indicated the aircraft's score of confirmed kills (*Walker*)

Kalamaki, in Greece, where the 96th FS's 2Lt Hiram C Pitts shot down a Bf 109.

It was back to Sofia on the 24th, this time escorting B-24s. Royal Bulgarian Air Force fighters intercepted them again, as a result of which Maj Litton (flying with the 96th FS) was credited with a Bf 109 destroyed and 1Lts Charles Hicks and Jack Walker of the 97th with two more probably destroyed. In 1998 a committee of the American Fighter Aces Association unofficially upgraded Walker's probable to a destroyed, giving him a total of five, and recognised him as an ace.

These long high-altitude missions were a challenge for the Lightning pilots. The combination of expanded cockpit time and the extreme cold made for a very uncomfortable experience, particularly as the heating system in the older model P-38s was notoriously inefficient. They also put a strain on the 82nd's dwindling inventory of war-weary F- and G-models, many of which were veterans of the North African campaign.

The group escorted Liberators to Greece on 6 December, their target being Eleusis airfield. They were greeted by enemy fighters, resulting in claims for four destroyed, two probables and two damaged, including two Bf 109 victories credited to 1Lt Leslie 'Andy' Andersen of the 96th FS. The 97th's 2Lt Gene H Chatfield, who was on his first combat mission (and who had never flown a P-38 prior to joining the 82nd two weeks earlier), was credited with an Fw 190 destroyed.

Four days later the group returned to Sofia with the B-24s, claiming nine enemy fighters destroyed, one probable and four damaged for the loss of one P-38. The 96th's 'Andy' Andersen shot down a Bf 109 for his fifth kill, thereby becoming the 82nd FG's 18th ace. His squadronmate 2Lt Hiram Pitts was the biggest scorer, with two Bf 109s downed and another probably destroyed. In the 97th, Capt Spencer, 1Lt Hicks and 2Lt Jorgensen were each credited with a Bf 109 destroyed and 1Lt Walker claimed an Fw 190 kill.

The 82nd's next aerial clash came on 20 December, again over Sofia. Around 24 enemy fighters opposed the bombers and the P-38s, and, according to the mission report, their pilots were 'definitely first class', which would seem to be confirmed by the fact that three of the Lightnings were shot down. The group produced matching claims of three destroyed and four damaged, the confirmed kills (all by the 97th FS) including a Bf 109 each for 1Lt Charles Hicks and 2Lt Donald T Foley. Hicks would complete his tour in early February with a score of three destroyed and two damaged in the air and two destroyed and one damaged on the ground.

Tragedy struck the 82nd FG on 21 December, but it was not combat related. Lt Col MacNicol was returning to Italy from England in a B-24 when it crashed on takeoff, killing him and others onboard. He had been advising the Eighth Air Force on the utilisation of its P-38s, which were just entering service there. Whilst he had made just one aerial (damaged) claim, MacNicol had destroyed five enemy aircraft on the ground to become a 'strafing ace'. He was replaced by his deputy, Bill Litton, who was promoted to lieutenant colonel in February.

The group experienced another disaster four days later, on Christmas Day, and this time it *was* combat related. During a B-24 escort to the marshalling yards at Udine, in Italy, Bf 109s attacked in the target area, utilising the hit-and-run tactics that had been so successful over Sofia five days earlier. The fight lasted 40 minutes, and by the time it was over six P-38s had gone down and two more were so badly damaged they had to be scrapped.

One of those killed was 95th FS CO Maj Hugh Muse, who was flying his P-38G-15 *TENNESSEE TODDY* (43-2428/'AM'). By a tragic coincidence, this was his 50th mission. Muse had scored one aerial victory, a single ground kill and claimed to have damaged another three enemy aircraft in the air and three on the ground. Also killed was the 96th FS's 2Lt Hiram Pitts (in P-38G-10 42-13130), who had been credited with three confirmed kills and two probables. Against these losses there was just one official claim, for a Bf 109 destroyed by Maj Litton, who was flying with the 96th.

The German pilots involved in this apparently one-sided engagement were from II./JG 51 and III./JG 53, which together claimed six P-38s. Oberleutnant Otto Schultz, the *Kommandeur* of 6./JG 51, who received credit for two of them, had fought against the 82nd FG in North Africa, where he claimed nine Lightnings destroyed. Schultz survived the war with 73 victories. Since the two *gruppen* reported losing three Bf 109s, it seems pretty certain that the 82nd pilots who were killed that day accounted for two victories that went unclaimed. Not coincidentally, the bomber crewmen witnessed at least three Bf 109s being shot down by the P-38s.

A B-17 escort was flown to Sofia on 4 January 1944, but this time there was little opposition. Indeed, the only claim was for a Bf 109 damaged. On the way home, over Yugoslavia, some 97th FS pilots spotted an He 111 bomber towing a Gotha Go 242 troop transport glider and shot them both down. Since seven pilots, including Lts Gene Chatfield and Bob Kinnie, hit the Heinkel, the official credit was given to the squadron as a whole (there was no separate credit for the glider).

FOGGIA

A notable event that month was the group's next move, from Lecce 150 miles north to Foggia No 11 (also called Vincenzo) which would be the 82nd's last wartime base. It was fully installed there by the 11th.

The group's first big mission from Foggia was on 14 January, and it took the form of a B-24 escort to Mostar, in Yugoslavia. As the formation left its target more than a dozen Bf 109s bounced the high (97th) squadron. 1Lt Paul Jorgensen and his wingman were jumped whilst in a turn and dove away. 'Jorgie' later recalled that 'we were hitting 550 mph on the way down, and I thought my aeroplane was going to fall apart'. After briefly blacking out, and then recovering from his dive, Jorgensen spotted a Messerschmitt on his wingman's tail and shot it down. Another Bf 109 then attached itself to *his* tail and hit both wings and booms and the cowling around the right supercharger. Fortunately, Jorgensen was able to out-turn it and escape. His P-38, named *Betty May* after his wife and coded 'C3', was badly damaged, but it brought him home. This was Jorgensen's final claim, and third confirmed kill. Two other enemy fighters were destroyed and two damaged. On the debit side, two P-38 pilots were killed.

Ten days later the group again visited Sofia with the B-24s. This time the formation was attacked well before the target, a dozen Bf 109s and

95th FS CO Maj Hugh Muse and his Lightning *TENNESSEE TODDY* (P-38G-15 43-2428/'AM') shortly before he was killed in it during the disastrous mission on Christmas Day 1943 (*Hugh Lee Thompson*)

Fw 190s making determined head-on passes at the bombers north of Skoplje, in Yugoslavia. The P-38 pilots immediately intervened and a lively dogfight ensued. The enemy gave as good as they got, the 82nd claiming two destroyed, one probable and three damaged for the loss of two Lightnings. Jack Walker made his final claim on this mission, for a Bf 109 destroyed, bringing his (official) total to four destroyed, three probables and one damaged. He finally completed his tour and went home in March.

Making his first claim that day was Capt Clayton M 'Ike' Isaacson of the 96th FS, who was credited with a probable Fw 190. Isaacson had joined the group in September after completing a tour as a B-25 pilot with the 321st BG, which the 82nd had often escorted. At 6 ft 6 in, he was one of the tallest pilots in the USAAF, and had originally been denied the opportunity to fly fighters because of his size. However, Isaacson was allowed to do so on his second combat tour. More than 50 years later, in a case similar to Jack Walker's, that same American Fighter Aces Association committee unofficially upgraded Isaacson's probable victory on 24 January to a destroyed, thus giving him a total of five kills and likewise recognising him as an ace.

On the 30th the 82nd participated in one of several Fifteenth Air Force missions in support of the new Anzio beachhead south of Rome, where landings had begun the week before. The targets were four airfields in northern Italy whose aeroplanes posed a threat to the Allied advances. The 82nd's task was to escort B-24s bombing Udine airfield.

Several dozen enemy fighters were encountered before, during and after the bombing. Many of them were quite aggressive, although considerably less successful than their 82nd FG opponents, who claimed six destroyed, five probables and two damaged for the loss of one P-38. Unfortunately, that loss was a big one, as the pilot of the Lightning was 97th FS CO Maj Charles Spencer, who was killed. Spencer had become separated from his wingman early in the fight and then went to the aid of the trailing bombers, which were being attacked by some Bf 109s. One of his pilots saw him shoot a fighter down (bringing his aerial score to three destroyed and two damaged) and then his Lightning, P-38G-10 42-13173, began 'smoking and going down slowly in a spiral as though it was out of control'. Spencer, who had assumed command of the 97th and been promoted to major just a week earlier, was awarded a posthumous Silver Star for this mission. He was succeeded as squadron CO by Capt Litchfield.

During February Italy experienced very poor weather, limiting the number of missions the 82nd could fly. Early that month it was decided that due to the continuing shortage of aircraft, all the group's P-38s

Paul 'Jorgie' Jorgensen (on the right) describes to Lts J D 'Don' Stoutenborough (on the left) and Bob Kinnie what happened to him over Yugoslavia on 14 January 1944, shortly after their return from that mission. Lt Jorgensen downed a Bf 109 for his third, and final, kill, but his P-38 (*Betty May*/'C3'), in the background, was badly shot up in return. Stoutenborough's victory total was two and one probable in the air and one destroyed on the ground, whilst Kinnie had three and one (unofficially) shared in the air (*Jorgensen*)

Lt Sammy McGuffin of the 97th FS is awarded the DFC by Brig Gen Charles W Lawrence, CO of the 47th BW, for shooting down two Bf 109s over northern Italy on 14 February 1944 and damaging a third. They made his (final) score four destroyed, one probable and two damaged in the air and one destroyed on the ground (*USAF*)

97th FS flight leader 1Lt Fred Phillips Jr and his P-38 *Mel* in the spring of 1944. He had just two aerial victories (plus three on the ground) to his name, so the four swastikas on the aeroplane's nose probably represented its score. Phillips claimed his second kill (a C.202) over northern Italy on 18 March. He went home in July with a total of 59 missions completed. The 82nd FG's Lightnings did not normally utilise aircraft numbers like the large '79' on *Mel's* nose, so it is possible that the fighter had previously served with either the 1st or the 14th FGs, which did (*Terry Massick*)

would comprise a single pool, and that most missions would be flown by just two squadrons utilising whatever aeroplanes were available, as had been the case a year earlier in North Africa.

The 82nd's first really eventful mission that month – at least for two of its pilots – was on the 14th when the group escorted B-24s targeting marshalling yards at Ferrara, in Italy. Some Bf 109s were encountered by a 97th FS flight that had become separated from the rest of the group at the rendezvous and ended up accompanying the wrong bomber formation. 1Lt Sammy McGuffin damaged one of two Messerschmitts that made a half-hearted pass at them. A short while later he experienced engine trouble and lost both his flight and quite a bit of altitude. Then, according to the succinct squadron war diary, 'he pulled out at 12,000 ft and tried to rejoin the flight. One ME 109, apparently having taken a pass at bombers, pulled up in front. Burst at 200 yards – ME went down in flames. Four other MEs came down and Lt McGuffin dove to the deck and chased them round a mountain. Three-fourths of way around met one ME head-on, missing him, but shot another ME down'. Another member of his flight also destroyed a Bf 109.

McGuffin completed his tour the following month and went home with a score of four destroyed, one probable and two damaged in the air and one destroyed on the ground. In 1945 he flew another P-38 tour in the Pacific with the 49th FG.

The 82nd saw considerable combat on 24 February during one of a series of joint Eighth and Fifteenth Air Force missions designated Operation *Argument* (more popularly known as 'Big Week') that had begun on 20 February, targeting the German aircraft industry. The 82nd's assignment on the 24th was to escort some 'Big Friends' home after they had bombed a factory at Steyr, in Austria. Coincidentally, the day before a new policy had gone into effect awarding double sortie credits to the pilots for extra-long missions like this one.

When the group's P-38s moved into position behind the last in the bombers over the target – B-17s of the 2nd BG – they were being attacked by a swarm of more than 100 single- and twin-engined fighters. The 82nd pilots immediately went to their aid, the ensuing fight resulting in claims for eight destroyed, two probables and three damaged. Amongst the claimants was 1Lt Gene Chatfield of the 97th FS, who downed an Me 410. His squadronmate 1Lt Fred Phillips was in a flight that made a pass at four of them. Phillips became separated from it, and upon discovering that one of his auxiliary fuel tanks had failed to drop, he headed for the deck, where he met an Me 410 head-on in a valley, fired a burst and saw it crash into a mountain.

Unfortunately, before the P-38s could come to its aid, the 2nd BG had lost a complete box of ten B-17s – 14 of the 16 bombers lost that day were from that one group. The 82nd FG likely saved it from complete annihilation. One of the pilots who made a claim following this action was the 95th FS's Flt Off Roland O 'Tuffy' Leeman, who shot down an Me 410 with *"THE SAD SACK"* (43-2112), which was now his assigned aircraft. In the 96th, 1Lt Charles H Pinson put in a claim for a Bf 109 that was credited to him as a probable. The group lost one P-38.

Bad weather continued to limit the 82nd FG's missions in March. The first air action that month was not until the 18th, during a fighter sweep by the 95th and 97th FSs, together with the 1st and 14th FGs, targeting Axis airfields in the Udine area. Although flying just 50 ft above the Adriatic, and maintaining strict radio silence, they failed to achieve surprise. As the 97th climbed during the approach to its target, the unit was bounced by 30 enemy fighters. The Lightning pilots quickly went into a huge 'Lufbery' with aircraft from the other two groups. Fred Phillips shot a C.202 off the tail of another P-38 and Don Foley destroyed a Bf 109 as it attempted to penetrate the circle. The only other claim was for a C.202 damaged. One 82nd P-38 was lost in return.

The next day's mission was also eventful, as the group again escorted B-17s to Austria. The bombers were attacked by enemy fighters over Yugoslavia en route, the 97th FS diving on the Axis machines as they climbed toward the 'Forts'. Two Fw 190s were downed (one of them by 1Lt John C Tate) and a Bf 109 damaged.

On 20 March the group finally received some new aircraft in the shape of its first P-38Js. They would continue to trickle in during the coming weeks, and more than two months would eventually pass before the 82nd had completely replaced its old F-, G- and H-models. Two of the P-38J's noticeable improvements were its greater range, due to an increased internal fuel capacity, and better cockpit heating. Appearance-wise the two major differences were the deeper air intakes below the propellers and the fighter's natural metal finish (no more camouflage paint). The J-models would fly their first combat mission on 29 March with the 96th FS.

The group's mission for 26 March – an escort for the B-17s attacking Steyr – was pretty much a repeat of the one a week before. Fifteen enemy

97th FS pilots pose with extremely colourful P-38G-13 43-2353, which was assigned to an unidentified captain sometime in early 1944. They are, from left to right, Lts Donald T Foley (who had two confirmed aerial victories, plus two destroyed on the ground), Wallace G Engh (one), John C Tate (three, plus one on the ground), William W 'Bill' Patterson (two), Fred Phillips (two, plus a probable and three on the ground) and John S Batie (three). Batie and Tate each claimed an Fw 190 over Yugoslavia on 19 March 1944. 43-2353 was destroyed in a crash-landing on 17 May that killed its pilot, 2Lt Dean Reinert (*Author*)

fighters attacked the bombers over Yugoslavia shortly after the rendezvous. Capt Litchfield's 97th FS and the 95th's spare flight were ordered to deal with them. They did so in a very efficient manner, claiming five destroyed, one probable and three damaged without loss. Litchfield scored the probable, his squadronmate Gene Chatfield his third, and last, aerial victory (another pilot had hit Lt Chatfield's victim first, but he received the sole official credit) and the 95th's 2Lt Melvin E Wiedbusch his first kill – all these claims were for Bf 109s. A Bf 110 was also destroyed and an Fw 190 damaged.

As of the following day, the 82nd FG was assigned to the Fifteenth Air Force's new 306th Fighter Wing (FW). In North Africa it had been attached to the 47th Bomb Wing (BW), and then in Italy to the 5th BW.

On 28 March the group participated in Operation *Strangle*, targeting Axis supply routes in northern Italy to reduce the flow of enemy troops and materiel to the now rather static front in the centre of the country below Rome. In this case the targets were the marshalling yards at Verona. Northwest of Ferrara, the high-cover P-47s of the 325th FG attacked 24 enemy fighters attempting to get behind the bombers. The 82nd's pilots also engaged some of them, the group leader, Capt Litchfield, climbing up to assist the Thunderbolts. Quickly latching onto a Bf 109, Litchfield chased it down in such a steep dive that his controls froze, causing him to consider bailing out. He finally managed to regain level flight at 3000 ft, having used every bit of his strength. Litchfield then spotted two more Bf 109s at his altitude, out-turned one of them and heavily damaged it. Moments later he saw the pilot of the Messerschmitt bail out at very low altitude. A C.202 was also shot down and another Bf 109 damaged.

The 82nd FG's last air combat in March, on the 30th, was over a familiar location – Sofia. And for the first time in many weeks all three squadrons were involved. Two flights of the 95th saw all the action when ten enemy fighters attacked the rear of the B-17 formation as it approached the target. They claimed five destroyed and two damaged, including two 'Me 309s', one of which was shot down by Flt Off Leeman in *THE SAD SACK*. As the Me 309 was an experimental type that never made it into frontline service, these were almost certainly French Dewoitine D.520s that the Germans had given to the Royal Bulgarian Air Force after confiscating them from the *Armée de l'Air*. The Bf 109 claimed by 2Lt Joseph F Belton Jr was the first of his eventual four victories.

30 March was also a memorable day for John Litchfield, but not for any combat or flying experience. Rather, he underwent an emergency appendectomy. This brought his tour to a premature end at 45 missions, with a score of two destroyed and one probable in the air and one destroyed and one damaged on the ground. Taking his place as CO of the 97th FS was Capt Claud Ford, who had originally been assigned to the 95th but transferred to the 97th as its new operations officer on 2 February.

The first mission in April was a return trip with the bombers to Steyr on the 2nd. The formation was once again attacked by enemy fighters over Yugoslavia en route, the 82nd's pilots subsequently claiming three

The 97th FS's Lt Gene Chatfield was photographed shortly after the 26 March 1944 bomber escort mission to Austria during which he claimed a Bf 109 destroyed for his third, and final, aerial victory. The aircraft in the background is one of the group's brand-new J-model Lightnings, 42-104054, which has yet to have its nose painted red (*Chatfield*)

destroyed, one probable and two damaged without loss. One of the victors was 1Lt Charlie Pinson of the 96th FS, who was awarded the Silver Star for his actions that day. According to the mission report, 'Some enemy aircraft dived through the high escort formation, evidently trying to get the P-38s to follow them down and get out of position'. One of the newer pilots took the bait and Pinson went to his rescue, as he remembered many years later;

'Six '109s came down out of the sun on the P-38. The "decoy" '109 made a tight turn, which brought the P-38 in front of his buddies. It also allowed me to turn in behind them. We were all in a daisy-chain turn, with them trying to shoot at the P-38 in front. The '109s evidently did not see me join the fight. With my first burst I hit the lead '109, which was closing on the P-38, and it exploded in a ball of red flame and black smoke. The other, startled, '109 pilots immediately pulled back up, except for the decoy, which split-S'd. The '109s quickly descended upon us again from different directions.

'Calling the new pilot by name and directing each break (left or right), I set up a two-ship weave pattern, covering each other. We turned into each attacking '109 for a head-on pass, sometimes in trail and sometimes going in opposite directions, and then quickly doing a 180 turn, passing by each other for another head-on shot should a '109 manage to get on one of our tails. This worked pretty well and the '109s didn't get any good deflection shots. Sometimes they broke off early, not wishing to complete a head-on pass against the concentrated firepower of the P-38s. We both took some single hits, and I saw one of my cannon shells explode on the prop of a '109, but no more decisive hits were made. After about 20 passes the '109s broke off the attack, climbing away into the sun.'

In the 97th, Capt Ford was credited with a probable Bf 109 and Lt Tate destroyed another and damaged an Fw 190.

On 3 April the 82nd FG participated in the first USAAF raid on Hungary, specifically Budapest. Some 24 Royal Hungarian Air Force fighters intercepted the American formation, and although they brought down several bombers they were not successful against the escorting P-38s. The 82nd's pilots claimed four destroyed and the 1st and 14th FGs another five.

1Lt Richard E Willsie of the 96th FS hit an Me 210 heavily and watched it hurtle earthward, apparently out of control. One of his squadronmates gave it another burst for good measure before it crashed. When they returned to

John Litchfield, one of the 95th FS's original staff sergeant pilots who transferred out in California, returned to the group in August 1943 but was assigned this time to the 97th. He destroyed a Ju 88 on the ground during the 18 September Foggia strafing mission, shot down a Bf 109 on 31 October and probably destroyed another on 26 March. When this photograph was taken of Capt Litchfield, his crew chief TSgt Robert Elkin and their P-38 *Sweet Pea*, he had just shot down a Bf 109 over northern Italy on 28 March 1944, two days before undergoing an emergency appendectomy that brought his tour to a premature conclusion (*USAF*)

2Lt Roland 'Tuffy' Leeman of the 95th FS scored his second kill (a Bf 109 over Hungary on 3 April 1944) in his famous P-38 *"THE SAD SACK"* (*Author*)

The 95th FS's Lt Melvin Wiedbusch is seen here with his P-38G-15 *BARBARA ANN* (43-2489/'A6') shortly after scoring his third confirmed kill over Hungary on 13 April 1944. Wiedbusch was killed in action on 25 June in his new P-38J (*Charles Adams*)

base it was decided that they should flip a coin to decide who received the official credit, and Willsie lost! Originally assigned to the 414th Night Fighter Squadron, flying British-supplied Bristol Beaufighters, Willsie transferred to the 82nd in mid-December and initially flew some experimental night intruder missions over northern Italy in a P-38.

The 97th's Capt Ford caught an 'Me 410' (actually a Hungarian licence-built Me 210) at very low altitude and shot it down. His wingman, 2Lt LeRoy L 'Lee' Lette, destroyed a Bf 110, whilst newly commissioned 2Lt 'Tuffy' Leeman of the 95th scored with *THE SAD SACK* again, downing a Bf 109.

The group visited another new Axis country on the 4th when it provided withdrawal support for B-24s that had bombed Bucharest, in Rumania. When the 95th FS pilots spotted the bombers, they were being attacked by some twin-engined fighters. Wading in, the Lightning pilots claimed three destroyed and a probable. One of the former, a Ju 88, was credited to 1Lt Tom Hodgson, who had just returned for his second combat tour (the first 82nd FG pilot to do so), of which this was his first mission, and another was a Bf 110 downed by 2Lt Harlon J 'Jake' Conger. Conger had joined the 95th in November and made his first claim, for a probable Bf 109, on 30 January.

The group flew another bomber escort to Vienna on 12 April. Enemy fighters were encountered in the target area and four were destroyed and one damaged, all by the 95th FS. Amongst the victors were 2Lts Conger and Wiedbusch, with an Fw 190 destroyed apiece.

The following day the 82nd returned with its 'Big Friends' to Budapest, providing target and withdrawal cover. It met 30 enemy fighters, of which the group's pilots claimed ten destroyed. Seven of the kills were by the 95th FS. 2Lt Charles E 'Chuck' Adams Jr (who was also nicknamed 'Bones' due to his thin physique) scored his first victory, an Me 210, in P-38G-10 42-13199/'AI', 2Lt Leeman claimed a Ju 88 with *THE SAD SACK*, 2Lt Paul R Mass downed another Ju 88 for his first kill (in P-38G-15 43-2434/'A-12', nicknamed *Margie*) and 2Lt Melvin Wiedbusch got a Bf 109 (his third). In the 96th, Capt Isaacson, who had been appointed squadron CO on 21 March, scored his first confirmed kill, an Me 210.

The group returned to Rumania on 16 April, but failed to rendezvous with the bombers. However, a lone He 111 was spotted 30 miles north of the Danube, and although it was hit by several 97th FS pilots before it crashed, future ace 2Lt Robert C Griffith was credited with its destruction as his first victory.

18 April brought a strafing mission to a landing ground near Aiello, in Italy. Due to the poor visibility over the target, only a few 97th FS pilots were able to do any

Lt Wiedbusch's squadronmate 2Lt Paul Mass scored his first victory on 13 April 1944, on only his second combat mission. He was flying his assigned P-38G-15 (43-2434/'A-12'), named *Margie*, which he continued to do until it had to be scrapped the following month and he received a new P-38J. By the time he completed his tour at the end of July, Mass had run his score up to four destroyed in the air and two on the ground (*Mass*)

real damage, claiming three aircraft destroyed and two damaged. One of the former was an unidentified biplane credited to 1Lt John Tate, while 1Lt Don Foley got a biplane and an Re.2000. Foley completed his tour in mid-May with two enemy aircraft destroyed in the air and these two on the ground to his credit. He opted to stay on in Italy for a while as assistant group operations officer.

The 82nd returned to Wiener Neustadt with the B-24s on 23 April. Although dozens of enemy fighters were seen over and near the target, the group had few opportunities to score as it was assigned to close cover. The 95th FS's 'Jake' Conger did manage to shoot down a Bf 109, and two others were damaged. The 95th downed two more enemy aircraft near Zagreb, Yugoslavia, on the way home, and then strafed a nearby airfield, claiming three destroyed and three damaged on the ground, one of which was a Ju 87 destroyed by Lt Conger.

It was back to Rumania on the 24th, and again the group's pilots did some strafing on the way home. At Kraljevo airfield in Yugoslavia, three enemy aircraft were destroyed on the ground by the 95th FS, including an Fi 156 and an He 111 by Lt 'Chuck' Adams. The following day, during a raid on the Macchi factory at Verese, in Italy, the 82nd's pilots protected the B-24s from determined attacks by some of their particularly aggressive and skilful enemy counterparts, a number of whom were Fascist Italians. The best they could do, however, was four

Maj Herbert L Phillips assumed command of the 95th FS on 21 March 1944 and scored his first aerial victory (an Fw 190 over southern France) on 29 April. Little is known about the very interesting P-38 in the background, other than that it had shot down 11 enemy aeroplanes, was named *My Lady* and was a G-model (*Author*)

damaged claims, all by the 95th, including a Bf 109 by 'Jake' Conger, for the loss of two of their own.

According to a squadron war diary entry for the 26th, Lt Conger 'was transferred to Wing for shooting off his mouth to the Colonel at last night's critique' of the day's mission. He completed his tour by flying 18 more P-38 missions with the 154th Weather Reconnaissance Squadron. Conger had been one of the 'hottest' pilots in the 95th before his transfer, with a score of three destroyed, one probable and one damaged in the air and one destroyed and one probable on the ground.

29 April brought a very long bomber escort to Toulon, in France. Four Fw 190s made a pass at some B-24s near the target and Maj Herb Phillips, who had been 95th FS CO since 21 March, managed to shoot one of them down.

A lot of the missions flown during May were tactical in nature, including support for Marshal Tito's forces in Yugoslavia. The group did escort some bombers to the marshalling yards at Verona, in Italy, on the 2nd, however. A few Bf 109s were encountered and one was shot down by 1Lt John Tate of the 97th FS, but the enemy downed a P-38 in return.

Four days later the 82nd provided penetration support for an attack by the 'heavies' on marshalling yards in Rumania. Some Bf 109s bounced the 96th FS shortly after the formation passed the Danube en route to the target. The 95th joined in, and the spirited dogfight that ensued ended up on the deck in many cases. The result was five of the Messerschmitts claimed destroyed for the loss of one P-38. Amongst the claimants was 2Lt Andrew M Blakely Jr of the 96th, with a single kill.

When the group returned to Wiener Neustadt on 10 May two large formations of Bf 109s were spotted, but the enemy seemed loath to engage. Two of the Messerschmitts did make a head-on pass at the 96th FS, and then 'split-S'd'. One of them was followed by the 97th FS flight led by Lt Col Ben A Mason, the group's new deputy CO, who remembered years later;

'The '109 immediately dove for the ground, our altitude at the time being about 20,000 ft. Instead of making a straight/steep dive, he made a series of cutbacks from left to right. We had tracers mixed in our ammunition, and I threw some short bursts from long range out in front of him a few times. Perhaps this is what made him turn. This allowed me to turn inside him a little each time, and to close faster. I remember looking at my airspeed and seeing it over 400 mph and close to the red line that we were not supposed to exceed. I didn't look at it again, as I wasn't about to slow down! We soon levelled out at about 100 ft. I was closing fast now, and firing a burst whenever I had him in my sights. I could see the 20 mm burst when it hit and knew four 0.50-cals were going in with it. I was about to slow down to keep from over-running him when he went in.'

On the way home more enemy aircraft were encountered by the 97th over Hungary, and an Fw 190 was shot down and an Me 410 damaged.

Deputy group CO Lt Col Ben Mason scored the first of his two aerial victories near Czelldomolk, in Hungary, on 10 May 1944. This photograph was taken after his second success, on 10 June. Mason named his P-38J-15 43-28778/'HB' *Billy Boy* after his young son (*Mason*)

Ben Mason had joined the group in early April, filling the position that had not been held officially since Bill Litton was promoted to group CO three months earlier. Mason had made a nuisance of himself to obtain a transfer to a combat assignment from his staff job with HQ, Mediterranean Allied Air Forces (MAAF). At 32, he was by far the oldest pilot in the 82nd.

The group received another airfield strafing assignment on 17 May. The targets were Villafranca and Ghedi in Italy's Po Valley – and specifically the Ju 88s that were based there. P-38s from the 95th FS swept across the fields in line abreast, destroying two of the Junkers and damaging three others. The two confirmed kills were credited to Maj Phillips and 2Lt Mass. Another Ju 88 was shot down.

The 82nd was supposed to have provided withdrawal support to bombers attacking the oil refineries at Ploesti, in Rumania, on the 18th, but when its 'Big Friends' did not show up at the rendezvous the group's P-38 pilots returned home, strafing two airfields in Yugoslavia on the way. This resulted in claims for one destroyed, one probable and two damaged on the ground and a Bf 109 damaged in the air. The confirmed kill, a Ju 52/3m, was by the 97th's 2Lt Bob Griffith. Eight days later there was a planned attack on Zemonico/Zara airfield in Yugoslavia, which the 96th and 97th FSs dive-bombed and strafed. Amongst the claims for three aircraft destroyed and four damaged was a Ju 52/3m credited to 2Lt Arthur W Kidder Jr of the 96th (claimed as destroyed).

Another large strafing mission to Yugoslavia was scheduled for 28 May, targeting four towns, a marshalling yard and three airfields (two of them at Banjaluka and the other at Livno), resulting in a high score of enemy aircraft. Some 34 were originally claimed destroyed, but due to many obvious duplications that number was later reduced to 18. Amongst the claimants in the 97th FS were 'Hank' Ford (a Fiat CR.42 biplane fighter) and Bob Griffith (two unidentified aircraft). 'Ike' Isaacson made the only strafing claim in the 96th, for an 'unidentified army co-op monoplane' (Ford and Isaacson had both received their promotions to major three days earlier). The 95th was by far the most successful squadron, with Lt Joe Belton claiming a CR.42 and an unidentified monoplane destroyed, Lt 'Tuffy' Leeman two CR.42s and an unidentified monoplane destroyed and Lt Tom Hodgson and Lt Jack D Joley two CR.42s destroyed apiece. Two Fi 156s were spotted in the air and shot down by the 96th's 2Lt Andy Blakely.

The next day proved to be just as productive. That morning, after providing penetration support for bombers en route to Wiener Neustadt, the group again strafed ground targets in Yugoslavia on its way home. The 95th FS hit an airfield south of Zagreb, destroying six enemy aircraft and damaging three more. The 96th then attacked Zara airfield, where three more were claimed destroyed, including a BR.20 by Lt Edward F Bodine and an Fi 156 by Lt Richard M Gangel.

This was the 183rd, and last, mission for the 95th's venerable *"THE SAD SACK"* (43-2112), which was flown by its assigned pilot for the past four months, Lt Roland 'Tuffy' Leeman. The fighter was badly damaged by flak over Yugoslavia, and Leeman had to belly-land it back

"THE SAD SACK" was photographed after its last, ultimately fatal, mission on 29 May 1944, and just before it was scrapped. Aside from the damage it sustained that day from Axis anti-aircraft fire (note the huge hole in its nose) and its subsequent crash-landing, 43-2112's appearance had changed dramatically since its early days in North Africa (*Author*)

at Foggia as the aeroplane's hydraulic system had been knocked out and he could not lower the landing gear. 43-2112 was subsequently scrapped.

Another mission was laid on that afternoon when 50 P-38s took off to escort B-24s to Yugoslavia and then do more strafing there. After leaving the bombers the 95th provided cover as the other squadrons hit two airfields (one of the Banjalukas and the Bihac landing ground). Seventeen enemy aircraft were claimed destroyed and two more damaged. Amongst the nine destroyed at Banjaluka, in the 97th FS Maj Ford claimed two unidentified biplanes, Lt Gene Chatfield another and Lt Bob Griffith an He 111. In the 96th, Lt Andy Blakely was credited with two unidentified single-engined aircraft destroyed plus the two damaged and Lt Pelton W Ellis an unidentified tri-motor destroyed. Two pilots (one from each squadron) were killed by ferocious anti-aircraft fire.

The other eight enemy aircraft were destroyed at Bihac, including a Henschel Hs 126 army cooperation aircraft apiece by Lts John Tate and Lee Lette of the 97th FS. Their squadronmate Fred Phillips was the day's top scorer with a C.202 and two Fi 156s destroyed. Another Fi 156 was encountered in the air and shot down. Lt Phillips, who was on his 55th mission, made his final pass despite having been wounded in the previous strafing run when his aeroplane was hit by flak. To make matters worse, Phillips had been all but blinded by coolant that had sprayed into his cockpit after the fighter was damaged. Nevertheless, he managed to make it back to Foggia. For this feat Phillips was awarded the Silver Star and, of course, a Purple Heart. He went home in July after completing 59 missions, having claimed two aircraft destroyed and one damaged in the air and three destroyed on the ground.

John Tate, the 97th's operations officer, had flown his 50th mission the previous day, but like many of the group's veterans, he volunteered for a few more sorties because of a temporary shortage of qualified pilots. He flew his 57th mission on 30 June and then went home with the rank of captain, having shot down three enemy aircraft and damaged three more, and also damaged one on the ground. Gene Chatfield took his place as the squadron's second-in-command.

The first tangible accomplishment by the group in June was on the 5th, during strafing attacks on the airfields at Ferrara and Poggia Renatico and other targets in northern Italy. The 96th FS made the only aircraft claims, for three Bf 109s destroyed and three damaged on the ground. Two of the former were by 1Lts Ed Bodine and Dick Gangel.

PLOESTI

The 82nd FG flew one of its toughest missions on 10 June 1944. The group's target that day was one of the oil refineries at Ploesti, in Rumania, that provided the Axis war machine in Europe with much of its vital fuel and lubricants. Numerous attempts by Allied bombers to destroy them, beginning with the disastrous low-level raid by B-24s from North Africa on 1 August 1943, had only been partially successful, and the oil still flowed from them to the Wehrmacht and the Luftwaffe. Someone had the idea of another low-level raid, this time by P-38 fighter-bombers. It was approved and the 82nd was given the job.

The plan was for the group's pilots, escorted by those of the 1st FG, to fly as low as possible and under strict radio silence, thereby hopefully surprising the defences (German and Rumanian fighter units, extensive flak batteries and smoke generators) and enabling them to hit their individual targets with pinpoint accuracy. Early that morning Lt Col Litton led 46 P-38s off from Vincenzo. Having rendezvoused with the 1st over the Adriatic, the formation crossed the sea and then the mountains of Yugoslavia, before hitting the deck as it entered the valley of the Danube.

East of Bucharest, the Lightning pilots met a 'procession' of enemy aircraft. Although they had been admonished not to engage any en route, in some cases it became unavoidable – or nearly so – and six were claimed by the 82nd FG pilots. 1Lt Merrill M Adelson of the 96th FS destroyed an Me 210 and an

The long and the short of it – Lt Cols Litton (left) and Mason were photographed together after the 10 June 1944 Ploesti dive-bombing mission. Behind them is Litton's *LUCKY LADY* (P-38J-15 42-104145/ 'HA'). Normally, the group CO and his deputy did not fly on the same missions, but an exception was made for this extremely important assignment (*Mason*)

He 111 and probably destroyed an unidentified single-engined fighter, whilst 95th CO Maj Herb Phillips probably destroyed an unidentified biplane. The 97th's 2Lt Lee Lette recalled years later that 'an Hs 126 observation aeroplane was high-tailing it to the east, about a half-mile off my nose to the right of our flight path. I swung out and, with ten times as much lead as you give the puck at No 8 skeet station, fired a couple of short bursts. Smoking, down he went into a pasture as I slid back into formation'. The escort pilots of the 1st FG encountered even more enemy aircraft, and some of them became involved in a huge dogfight with Rumanian IAR fighters.

Four miles south of Ploesti the 82nd FG pilots began climbing to reach their bombing altitude. Unfortunately, surprise had not been achieved, but despite the smoke and a 'terrific and accurate barrage of light and heavy flak', the dive-bombers did considerable damage to the Romana Americana refinery. At least three of the eight pilots who were listed as missing in action following this mission fell to flak batteries there. One of them was the 95th FS's 1Lt Tom Hodgson (in P-38J-15 43-28688), who crash-landed after both his engines were hit. He was quickly taken prisoner, bringing his second tour to an abrupt conclusion. Hodgson's final score was three destroyed, one probable and two damaged in the air and three destroyed on the ground.

Many of the pilots who made it past the refinery did some strafing on the way home, and several of them encountered enemy aeroplanes. In the 96th, Lt Adelson added two Ju 88s destroyed on the ground to those he had claimed in the air earlier that day. After returning to Italy he crash-landed his P-38 at Crotone. Adelson's squadronmate 2Lt Walter J Carroll Jr shot down a Bf 109. Lt Col Mason was leading one of the 97th FS flights in P-38J-15 43-28778, which was coded 'HB' (indicating the deputy CO's aircraft) and named *Billy Boy* after his son. Having refrained from firing at a Bf 110 he had encountered prior to the bombing, he did not pass up a second opportunity when he spotted another Bf 110 coming in for a landing at an airfield he was strafing and shot it down.

Besides the damage to the refinery and other facilities and materiel, the group claimed eight destroyed, two probables and one damaged in the air and four destroyed and three damaged on the ground. It was awarded its third DUC for this mission.

On 14 June the 82nd flew a fighter-bomber mission to Kecskemet airfield in Hungary, which was a stopover point for transport aeroplanes flying fuel from the Ploesti refineries to Germany. The 95th FS hit the airfield first, destroying most of the aircraft on it – six huge, six-engined Me 323 transports, an Fi 156 and a Bf 109. Maj Phillips and 2Lts Jack Joley, Roy I Harman and James D Holloway each claimed one of the transports, while the latter pilot was also credited with the Fieseler. The other two squadrons then joined in and all but destroyed the facility.

The group's next air action came on the 16th during a B-24 escort to Vienna. When the formation was about 40 miles north of Lake Balaton, in Hungary, two Bf 109s attacked a 95th FS flight from above. The Lightning pilots dove after the Messerschmitts, whereupon two Fw 190s latched onto them. Thus began a 40-mile running fight that ended up over an airfield thought to be Veszprem, home of the Royal Hungarian Air Force's 101st 'Puma' Fighter Group, where the 95th encountered 12 more enemy fighters. The claims from this action, totalling eight destroyed and one damaged, included an Fw 190 by Chuck Adams. According to his combat claim report, 'Lt Adams met an enemy aircraft at 15,000 ft and he did a "split-S", so Lt Adams followed him down. He pulled out of his dive at about 500 ft and Lt Adams pulled out on his tail, but out of range. Throwing everything to the firewall, Lt Adams closed in and gave him several good squirts. He nosed down, hit the ground and blew up'. Adams was flying P-38J-15 43-289654/'AZ'.

'Tuffy' Leeman, who was leading the 95th that day, downed a Bf 109 and damaged an Fw 190. According to the group war diary, Lt Leeman 'narrowly missed becoming an ace when his guns jammed' whilst he was still shooting at the Focke-Wulf. These turned out to be his last claims, which totalled four destroyed and four damaged in the air and three destroyed and one shared probable on the ground. Amongst the other claimants were 2nd Lts Jim Holloway (an Fw 190) and Jack Joley (two Bf 109s). Three of their squadronmates were missing in action.

Six days later, during a bomber escort to the marshalling yards at Parma, in Italy, some of the group's pilots became involved in a tough fight over the Po Valley with what the mission report described as some 'aggressive and skilful' C.202 and Bf 109 pilots. The only claims were by the 96th FS, for a C.202 probably destroyed by 1Lt Merrill Adelson and another Macchi and a Bf 109 damaged. A 97th FS pilot was listed as missing in action.

The Joley twins (Jack, on the left, and Bob) were both pilots in the 95th FS, but with very different fates. Bob was killed in a flying accident at Foggia on 13 April 1944, whilst Jack returned home to his family in Michigan that summer with four confirmed aerial victories (the first two a pair of Bf 109s over Hungary on 16 June) and another four destroyed on the ground. He named his P-38 *Little Jo* after his baby daughter. The Lightning in the background – brand-new P-38J-15 43-28426 – has yet to receive its red nose. Also, note the 'Mr Bones' patches on the A-2 jackets (*Author*)

77

The 95th FS's Lt Jim Holloway became an ace when he shot down a Bf 110 and two Me 410s during the B-24 escort to Vienna on 26 June 1944. He would claim a Bf 109 on 2 July for a total of six victories (*Col Richard Willsie*)

Twenty-year-old 1Lt Bob Griffith of the 97th FS scored his third and fourth kills over Hungary on 2 July 1944, shortly before this photograph was taken of him and his P-38J-15 43-28679. The real 'Sweet Sue' was Griffith's mother. Having become an ace on 8 July, he was then shot down and killed in this aeroplane by Rumanian Air Force Bf 109s 16 days later. Griffith's final score was five destroyed, one probable and two damaged in the air plus seven destroyed on the ground, the latter an 82nd FG record (*M D Griffith*)

The 82nd's next big mission was on 24 June when the group escorted B-24s that were targeting more marshalling yards, this time at Craiova, in Rumania. Five Bf 109s were seen attacking a lone bomber at the rendezvous point, and the 95th FS went to its aid, downing three of the Messerschmitts (credited to 2Lts Joe Belton, Roy Harman and Jim Holloway) and damaging one. The 96th attacked another group of Messerschmitts and destroyed four more, including single victories by Maj Isaacson and 1Lts Walt Carroll and Charlie Pinson.

The following day the group returned to southern France, accompanying Liberators sent to bomb oil refineries. A dozen Bf 109s were encountered, but the result was only two damaged, against the loss of the 95th FS's 1Lt Melvin Wiedbusch (in P-38J-15 43-28774), who was last seen diving into clouds on the tail of a Bf 109. He was eventually declared killed in action, with a final score of three destroyed and one damaged.

The 82nd became involved in another big fight on the 26th during a long mission to Vienna. As its pilots approached the border of Hungary and Austria 40 to 50 twin-engined fighters and a few Bf 109s attacked the bombers. The 95th was the highest scoring squadron in the ensuing action, with claims totalling nine destroyed and seven damaged. 2Lt Jim Holloway claimed a Bf 110 and two Me 410s destroyed, thus taking his tally to five victories and making him an ace (the 19th in the 82nd FG). Maj Warner F Gardner, who had been assigned to the 95th 12 days earlier and would soon be appointed its new operations officer, was credited with two Bf 110s destroyed and another damaged. Maj Herb Phillips destroyed an Me 410 and damaged six(!) others, 1Lt 'Chuck' Adams (in P-38J-15 43-28796/'AI', which he had named *Judy Ann* after his daughter) downed a Bf 110 and 2Lt Paul Mass (in P-38J-15 43-28754/'A12') claimed both an Me 410 and a Bf 109.

The 96th FS scored three confirmed kills, including an Me 410 by 1Lt Ed Bodine and a Bf 109 by Capt Dick Gangel. The 97th got two, one of them an Me 410 (plus two more damaged) credited to 2Lt Bob Griffith. The group's grand total was 14 destroyed and nine damaged.

Paul Mass later described his victory over the Bf 109, which in many other USAAF fighter units would have been a shared kill;

'Lt [Barry] Butler was on the tail of an Me 109 that was turning sharply to the right. He was scoring hits on the fuselage and wings of the enemy aircraft. I could see the bursting cannon shells and the tiny bright flashes of the "fifties" as they hit.

'As I approached, the '109 manoeuvred in a manner that enabled me to fire a long burst from about 20 degrees down to near 0 degrees deflection, also scoring hits. As the angle neared 0 degrees I saw the '109's prop start to windmill and the pilot jettison his canopy. I stopped firing when I saw that happen. The '109 pilot pushed himself up until his head and upper torso were above the top of the fuselage. He threw his left leg over the side of the cockpit and rolled out head first. I was about 100 yards behind at this point. He did a half somersault in the air, coming straight toward me. I thought, "He's going into my left prop!" He passed feet first and face up at what looked to be a foot or so from the prop. I saw him go by between the left engine and the fuselage. I am sure he also thought he was going to hit my aircraft.'

Two 82nd pilots were lost that day, one of whom was the victim of Lt Pál Irányi, a Bf 109 pilot of the Hungarian 'Puma' Group. This was the third of his eventual six victories.

The 82nd's next major action was on 2 July, once again over Hungary, whilst escorting B-17s to an oil refinery there. Just before the target 30 twin-engined fighters were spotted, and followed, as they dove through a break in the overcast. 97th FS CO 'Hank' Ford shot down a lagging Bf 110, but the rest were lost in haze. By then the bombers were calling for help after being bounced from above. A mixed gaggle of Bf 109s and Fw 190s attacked the P-38s as they climbed back up, six of which (and no Lightnings) were shot down over and near Lake Balaton. This was part of a huge air battle involving units of both the Fifteenth and Eighth Air Forces, the latter's whilst flying from Italy during an Operation *Frantic* 'shuttle' mission from England to that country and Russia.

Maj Ford also shot down a Bf 109, the other 97th pilots making destroyed claims for Messerschmitts including 1Lts Robert A Biggs (one) and Bob Griffith (two). The squadron's total was five destroyed and one damaged. In the 95th, Maj Gardner and Lt Holloway were credited with an Fw 190 and a Bf 109 destroyed, respectively. Jim Holloway completed his combat tour the following day with a total of six destroyed and one damaged in the air and two destroyed and one damaged on the ground. He later served with the 459th FS in Burma, where he was killed in action (in P-38L-5 44-24245) on 18 June 1945.

4 July brought a change of pace, the 82nd being assigned a fighter sweep to Rumania. Three Ju 52/3ms with mine detonating rings that were spotted flying low over a river northwest of Craiova were shot down by 96th FS pilots Dick Gangel, Walt Carroll and Art Kidder.

The group returned to Hungary on the 7th as escorts for Liberators returning home after bombing targets in Germany. A section (two flights) from the 96th bounced four Bf 109s spotted at low altitude 70 miles north of Lake Balaton. The Lightnings were in turn jumped

Lt Arthur W Kidder Jr scored the first of his four confirmed aerial victories on 4 July 1944 when 96th FS pilots shot down three Ju 52/3m mine-laying aircraft near Craiova, in Rumania. In this photograph Kidder (standing, to left) is checking over his P-38J-10 42-67950/'BS' with his crew chief. Kidder flew another Lightning tour with the 54th FS in the Aleutian Islands the following year. 42-67950 was lost in action on 15 November and its pilot, 2Lt Lindsay Bowen, killed (*Walter Carper*)

by six more Bf 109s and then joined by the rest of their squadron. Two of the Messerschmitts were shot down, by 1Lts Walt Carroll and Merrill Adelson. The 95th then became involved in a skirmish with some other Bf 109s and claimed three destroyed, including one each to 1Lts Joe Belton (who was both squadron and group leader that day) and Jack Joley. One of its pilots was lost in this action.

The mission to which the group was assigned on 8 July was outstandingly successful, resulting in its second-largest one-day and one-mission score of enemy aircraft destroyed in the air (the largest

Lt Col Litton (second from left) congratulates 95th FS operations officer 1Lt Joseph F Belton Jr for scoring what was determined to have been the group's 500th confirmed aerial victory, over Hungary on 7 July 1944. The other pilots are Lts Merrill Adelson (on the left) and Walt Carroll, both of the 96th, who, like Belton, each scored a Bf 109 that day. Coincidentally, it was the third kill for all three of them. Belton's final total was four in the air and two on the ground, Adelson claiming the same, plus two probables. Carroll would soon be an ace (USAF)

being the haul on 11 April 1943). It was a rare – for the 82nd – fighter sweep, the group flying ahead of the bombers (sent to attack Vienna) in an effort to destroy enemy fighters that had been scrambled to intercept the 'Big Friends'. The group was led by 1Lt Charles Pinson at the head of the 96th FS, whilst the 95th FS was led by 1Lt Charles Adams and the 97th by 1Lt Robert Griffith. Twenty miles from the target, a large number of Me 410s were seen climbing for altitude, whereupon Pinson ordered a 'pincer' movement, with the 95th attacking from the left and the 96th from the right as the 97th provided top cover. The result was an aerial massacre, and a score of 19 destroyed, one probable and three damaged.

'Chuck' Adams (in P-38J-15 44-23188/'AE') shot down three of the Me 410s for a total of six kills and the 96th's 1Lt Walt Carroll had an identical score – Adams completed his tour on 2 August, with two enemy aircraft claimed destroyed on the ground in addition to those in the air. Amongst the others making claims for the twin-engined *Zerstören* were Maj Gardner (one destroyed, another probably destroyed and a third

Lts Art Kidder of the 96th FS (left) and Chuck Adams of the 95th (who were both from Denver, Colorado) congratulate each other for scoring three kills apiece during the aerial massacre over Vienna on 8 July 1944. These gave Adams a total of six, making him an ace, and Kidder his final total of four (USAF)

For this publicity shot Lt Adams points to his final score on the nose of his P-38J-15 43-28796/'Al' *Judy Ann*, which he named after his infant daughter. He scored just one of these victories in this aircraft – his fourth, a Bf 110 near Pozsony, in Hungary, on 26 June 1944 (*Adams*)

Lt Dick Willsie of the 96th FS and his colourful P-38J-15 42-104174/'Bl' *SNAKE EYES* after the 26 July 1944 *Frantic 3* mission from the Ukraine to Italy, during which he scored his only confirmed aerial victories – a Bf 109 and a Ju 52/3m transport. Willsie was a prewar body builder, long before that sport achieved mainstream popularity (*Willsie*)

damaged) and 1Lt Jack Joley (one destroyed) in the 95th, and the 96th's 1Lt Pelton Ellis (with the same score as Gardner), Capt Dick Gangel, 1Lt Art Kidder and Lt Pinson (the latter three pilots with one destroyed each).

97th FS pilots claimed two fighters destroyed, namely a Bf 109 by Lt Griffith and an Fw 190 by 1Lt Lee Lette, and damaged another whilst providing cover for their compatriots. This was Griffith's fifth confirmed victory – he, Adams and Carroll were the group's newest aces.

SHUTTLING

On 20 July the 96th FS's Maj Isaacson claimed one of two Bf 109s shot down during a B-17 escort to Memmingen, in Germany. Two days later the 82nd FG flew its first Operation *Frantic* 'shuttle' mission to Russia. This one was *Frantic 3*, and it was comprised of fighters only – P-38s of the 14th and 82nd FGs and P-51s of the 31st FG. By briefly flying from Russian bases, Eighth and Fifteenth Air Force units could reach enemy targets (specifically airfields in Rumania and Poland) that would be out of their range from England and Italy.

The 82nd's assigned targets en route to the Ukraine on 22 July were the airfields at Buzau and Zilistea, in Rumania. Its pilots did the strafing whilst the other two groups covered them. These attacks were spectacularly successful, with 41 enemy aircraft being claimed destroyed and nine damaged on the two airfields and their three satellite landing grounds.

Part of the 96th FS hit Buzau, and amongst those making claims totalling four destroyed and one damaged were Capt Dick Gangel (an unidentified biplane), 1Lt Charlie Pinson (an Fw 190 and an He 111 damaged) and 1Lt Dick Willsie (a Go 242 glider). Other 96th pilots attacked Zilistea, claiming eight destroyed and one damaged. They included the day's top scorer, Lt Thomas R Rosier, with an unidentified twin-engined bomber, a Bf 109, a Ju 87 and an Fi 156 destroyed, and Lt Pelton Ellis, with one unidentified single-engined aircraft destroyed.

A portion of the 97th FS also targeted Zilistea, where its pilots were credited with ten destroyed and four damaged, including destroyed claims for a Bf 109 and an Me 210 by Maj Ford, two Bf 109s by Maj Paul J Greene, two Fw 190s and an He 111 by 1Lt Bob Griffith and two Ju 88s by 1Lt Lee Lette. Other 97th pilots were very productive over the landing grounds to the tune of 13 destroyed and three damaged. Lt Col Mason claimed a Ju 52/3m, an unidentified single-engined

aircraft and an Fi 156 destroyed, while Lt Bob Biggs destroyed a Ju 52/3m and two Ju 88s.

Maj Greene, the assistant group operations officer, had been assigned to the 82nd in June. In 1941-42 he had served in China and Burma with the American Volunteer Group (AVG), with whom he had scored two destroyed, one probable and one damaged in the air.

The 95th FS claimed six destroyed and one damaged on the landing grounds, including two He 111s destroyed by Lt Roy Harman and another by Lt Paul Mass (once again flying 43-28754).

The group's pilots also caught a few enemy aeroplanes in the air, the claims for which totalled five destroyed, one probable and two damaged. Three Ju 52/3ms were shot down in Zilistea's traffic pattern, one of them by the 95th's Capt Joe Belton and another by Lt Biggs, whilst Lt Mass destroyed an He 111 that had just taken off. A flight of Fw 190s attacked some of the 97th's pilots as they left the area on the deck, Bob Griffith probably destroying one and Lee Lette (who was flying his 50th mission) shooting down one and damaging another. Lette recalled this fight some years later;

'As our airspeed dropped off after passing the field, I called out five bogies at "four o'clock". We turned into them and it started. After many turns, right and left – and a lot of yelling from everyone – I finally found an Fw 190 on the tail of my wingman, 1Lt John R Griffin. Desperate to get him off, I did my best to get there in time. The '190 finally broke away and I managed to out-turn him on the deck by utilising the manoeuvre flaps. He rolled over and hit the ground on fire. Immediately, I closed in on Griffin, who was having trouble keeping his P-38 level. He failed to respond to my yell to pull up and get out. As I passed over him his right wing flamed and separated just outside the engine nacelle. He flipped over and hit the ground from around 100 ft.'

Whilst heading northeast, alone, Lette saw two more Fw 190s above him, which he attacked head-on. He hit one of them in its nose 'with about 20 rounds' and then ran out of ammunition – it was smoking when he last saw it. He always believed his second Focke-Wulf was ready to crash, and would have for sure if he had had a little more ammunition. If Lette had been able to confirm its demise this would have been his fifth kill, and the group would have had another ace.

Two 96th FS pilots were also missing in action.

The 14th FG encountered a lot more enemy aircraft, claiming ten destroyed, five probables and nine damaged for the loss of two P-38s, whilst the 31st's P-51 pilots claimed four destroyed without loss.

On 25 July, flying from its temporary base at Poltava, the 82nd FG strafed Mielec airfield in western Poland with the 14th FG, the 31st FG providing cover for them. Unfortunately, the 82nd's pilots were out of position when they hit the airfield and had no aircraft targets, although some of the 14th's did and claimed a dozen destroyed. The group did encounter a few aircraft in the air, however, claiming three destroyed, including a Ju 87 by the 95th's 1Lt Roy Harman, bringing his total to two victories in the air and three on the ground. This aeroplane must have been one of those missed by the 31st FG, its pilots having claimed 19 Ju 87s destroyed after encountering a large formation of dive-bombers. The 31st FG was also credited with having downed six other enemy aircraft as well.

1Lt Charles Pinson became a PoW (temporarily) after he was shot down over Rumania in this aircraft (P-38J-15 42-104179/'BO', which he named *Penny II* after his sister) on 26 July 1944. The three victory markings denote the Bf 109 he shot down on 2 April, another Bf 109 on 24 June and an Me 410 over Vienna on 8 July. Pinson also scored a probable in the air and destroyed one aircraft on the ground (*Pinson via Warren Thompson*)

The three groups returned to Italy the following day, sweeping the Ploesti/Bucharest area en route. Near Galati, in Rumania, an Me 410 was spotted and the 96th's Maj Isaacson shot it down. The 82nd's P-38s were then attacked from above by single-engined fighters, initiating a huge 20-minute dogfight at low-level that resulted in a further nine enemy aircraft being shot down and three damaged. 96th FS pilots Capt Dick Gangel and 1Lts Ed Bodine and Dick Willsie were each credited with a Bf 109 destroyed, while 1Lt Pelton Ellis claimed two Messerschmitts and 1Lt Walt Carroll an Fw 190. The 97th downed two Bf 109s (claimed by Maj Ford and 1Lt Bob Biggs) and two damaged. Also, a Ju 52/3m and an He 111 were spotted taking off from the airfield at Manesti and quickly downed by Willsie and the 95th's Maj Gardner.

The victories for Gardner and Ford took their respective tallies to five, making them the 82nd FG's 23rd and 24th – and last – aerial aces. Carroll's success gave him a final score of seven destroyed and one probable. He returned to the USA the following month and subsequently became an instructor in California, where he was killed in a flying accident in P-38L-5 44-25807 on 20 January 1945.

The two pilots lost on this mission were unfortunately amongst the group's best. 1Lt Bob Griffith was shot down and killed in his P-38J-15 *Sweet Sue* (43-28679) by Bf 109 pilots of the Royal Rumanian Air Force's 9th Fighter Group, having fought alone against overwhelming odds before he finally went down. Griffith had volunteered to fly many more than his required 50 missions – this was his 63rd. He was credited with five destroyed, one probable and two damaged in the air and seven destroyed on the ground (the most strafing victories by any 82nd FG pilot) prior to his death.

The 82nd FG's leaders enjoy a game of cards at Vincenzo in late July. They are, from left to right, group CO Lt Col Bill Litton, 95th FS CO Maj Herb Phillips, 96th FS CO Maj Clayton Isaacson and 97th FS CO Maj Claud Ford (*Isaacson*)

The other pilot lost was the 96th's 1Lt Charlie Pinson, whose final score was three destroyed and one probable in the air and one destroyed on the ground. The right engine of his P-38J-15 42-104179/'BO', nicknamed *Penny II* after his sister, was knocked out when his flight was bounced by Bf 109s. With only one functioning motor, he opted to return to Poltava, which was closer than Italy, but he was attacked again by more Bf 109s and forced to crash-land, thus becoming a PoW.

The 14th FG also lost a P-38 whilst downing two Ju 52/3ms and the 31st's pilots claimed six Bf 109s without loss.

On 30 July the 82nd returned to Budapest with some B-24s, and Maj Greene from Headquarters, flying with the 97th FS, downed an Fw 190.

The group began another shuttle mission (*Frantic 4*) on 4 August. This one was also an all-fighter affair, and it included P-51s from the 52nd FG. En route to Russia, the 82nd strafed the Rumanian fighter base at Focsani, where five aircraft were destroyed and four damaged, including an unidentified transport and an unidentified single-engined aircraft by Lt Col Mason, who was flying with the 97th FS as usual.

The flak over Focsani was brutal, and it took a heavy toll. The 96th's 1Lt Dick Willsie had to make a forced-landing and, famously, was picked up by his squadronmate Flt Off Dick Andrews, Willsie then flying them both to Russia. A Bf 109 that tried to interfere was shot down by 1Lt Nathanial A 'Nate' Pape of the 95th and two others were damaged (the group also claimed a Ju 88 shot down). Unfortunately, Lt Col Litton, for whom this was, ironically, his 50th mission, was hit during the

The 95th FS's Lt Nathanial A 'Nate' Pape scored his only confirmed victory when he shot down a Bf 109 that was threatening the famous Andrews/Willsie rescue in Rumania – and damaged another – on 4 August 1944. He had previously scored a probable and made three other damaged claims. 'Nate' Pape's *Peg O' My Heart* was P-38J-15 43-28769/'AL' (*Author*)

Lt Col Litton (on the left) consults with Fifteenth Air Force commander Maj Gen Nathan Twining prior to taking off on the ill-fated (for him) *Frantic 4* shuttle mission on 4 August 1944, which was his 50th and, as it turned out, his last sortie (*USAF*)

approach to one of the airfields and his P-38J-15 42-104145 (which was named *Lucky Lady* and coded 'HA') was seen to crash into buildings and explode. It was assumed that he had been killed, but despite being badly injured Litton survived to become a PoW. Three other P-38s were also lost to the flak, while the 52nd FG claimed two aerial kills and lost four P-51s.

The group returned to Foggia on 6 August, strafing targets of opportunity on the way and destroying one enemy aircraft on the ground. This brought to an end an extremely eventful, and productive, period in the 82nd FG's history.

LETDOWN

After the group's last shuttle mission in early August 1944, its pilots' opportunities to engage enemy aircraft declined dramatically. This was partly due to the heavy losses the Axis air forces in southern and eastern Europe had suffered at the hands of the Fifteenth Air Force, but also because their attention was now focused primarily on other, more imminent, threats to the east and west. During the remaining eight months of the war in Europe the 82nd would claim a total of only four enemy aircraft destroyed in the air and 12 on the ground.

Many of the group's more successful pilots completed their tours around this time. They included Bob Biggs of the 97th FS, who had been credited with two enemy aircraft destroyed in the air and another four on the ground, and his squadronmate Lee Lette (four air and three ground). Also heading home were Ed Bodine (two air and three ground) and Dick Gangel (four air and two ground) of the 96th and, in the 95th, Roy Harman (two air and three ground), Jack Joley (four air and four ground) and Paul Mass (four air and two ground).

The only additional claims in August were for two Ju 88s damaged on the ground on the 13th by Majs Gardner and Greene, and a C.202 damaged in the air by Gardner on the 26th. 'Warnie' Gardner had taken over command of the 95th FS from Maj Herb Phillips on the 12th (the latter's final score including two confirmed aerial victories and two destroyed on the ground). Maj Ford, who had five aerial and five ground kills to his name, turned the 97th FS over to Paul Greene that same day. Greene, who had added one aerial victory and two destroyed and one damaged on the ground to his two destroyed, one probable and one damaged in the air with the AVG, was then still group operations officer, and he filled both positions for a while.

On 29 August Maj 'Ike' Isaacson relinquished command of the 96th FS to his operations officer, Capt Dick Willsie. He had been

95th FS CO Maj Gardner (right) poses with two of his (unidentified) groundcrewmen and his P-38J *LITTLE BUTCH V*, whose serial number and squadron code are unfortunately not known. 'Warnie' Gardner made his last aircraft claims during August, for a total of five destroyed and two damaged in the air and one damaged on the ground (*Author*)

The new Group CO Col Clarence 'Curly' Edwinson (on the left) greets the 82nd FG PoWs who were repatriated from Rumania at the end of August 1944. They are Capts Tom Hodgson, Charlie Pinson and Elwyn H Jackson, Lt Thomas W Vaughan and Col Bill Litton, the latter two men displaying evidence of their serious wounds. Tommy Vaughan had scored one aerial victory, as had his (95th) squadronmate Capt Jackson, although the latter's was over New Guinea early in the war while flying P-39s with the 35th FG. Jackson also had two ground kills with the 82nd FG and Vaughan four. Col Litton, with a DSC, two Silver Stars, a DFC, 12 Air Medals and a Purple Heart, was the group's most highly decorated pilot (*Jerome Loewenberg*)

credited with four confirmed aerial victories and one on the ground, and received the Silver Star. Isaacson was not finished yet, however, as he flew another tour as a P-38 squadron commander with the 49th FG in the Philippines. Willsie was promoted to major before he too finally went home in mid-December, having flown his 82nd, and last, mission on the 6th of that month – a group record he shared with 97th FS ace Gerry Rounds. Willsie's final claim was a transport aircraft damaged by strafing on 1 November, bringing his victory total to two destroyed and one damaged in the air and one destroyed and one damaged on the ground, although he had also lost a sure aerial kill to an unlucky coin toss.

With Rumania having capitulated to Soviet forces, the USAAF PoWs in that country were evacuated to Italy at the end of August. Amongst them were eight 82nd FG pilots, including Bill Litton and Capts Tom Hodgson and Charlie Pinson. Litton found that he had been promoted to full colonel whilst being held in captivity, and he was awarded both the DSC (for his bravery on the 4 August shuttle mission) and his second Silver Star. Col Litton's final score was two enemy aircraft destroyed in the air and two on the ground.

As summer turned to autumn, with nary an enemy aircraft in sight, few of the 82nd's air combat veterans remained at Foggia. Deputy group CO Lt Col Ben Mason flew his final mission in mid-October, and on the 26th of that month both Maj Gardner and Lt Col Greene left the group, the latter moving up to HQ of the new 305th FW, which oversaw the Fifteenth Air Force's three P-38 groups. Mason, who had scored two kills in the air and five on the ground, was also a Silver Star recipient. Gardner, with five victories, had been the last ace still flying with the group. The 97th's Gene Chatfield had extended his tour, for which he was rewarded

Capt John 'Pappy' Tate (on the left) began his second combat tour as 97th FS CO Lt Col Paul Greene was completing his first. Tate scored three kills in the air and two on the ground during his first USAAF tour, also with the 97th. This time he would be assistant group operations officer. Greene, who had also been group operations officer, was a former 'Flying Tiger' who scored two destroyed, one probable and one damaged in the air over Burma in 1941-42. With the 82nd he claimed one destroyed in the air and two on the ground (*Author*)

with a captaincy, but he returned home in September after an attack of appendicitis with a score of three and one (unofficially) shared victories in the air and one on the ground. He also received his award of the Silver Star that month.

Even as these men left the group, it began to welcome back some of its veteran pilots for another tour. Among them was Capt John Tate, who was assigned to group operations in November. Another was 1Lt Fred Phillips, whose second tour with the 97th FS ended in tragedy when he was killed in a flying accident in P-38L-1 44-24135 on 7 December.

A 95th FS pilot scored a very unusual aerial victory on 29 October, receiving official credit for shooting down a lone, early-model P-51 (determined to have been a captured, enemy-operated aircraft) that had opened fire on one of his squadronmates over Austria. Enemy aeroplanes were also occasionally encountered in the autumn and winter months during the frequent escorts for Fifteenth Air Force F-5 photo-reconnaissance Lightnings ('Photo Freddies'), these unarmed machines often being intercepted by the Luftwaffe's new Me 262 jet fighters. The group's pilots damaged four Me 262s and a Bf 109 during these missions.

Ironically, the 82nd's biggest aerial battle during this period was with some Allied fighters. This infamous incident took place on 7 November during a typical fighter-bomber mission led by the group CO, Col Clarence Edwinson. Sent to attack retreating German columns in Yugoslavia, the P-38 pilots shot up a truck convoy in the wrong valley that turned out to be Russian, killing, among many others, a Soviet general! Some Yak fighters then took off from a newly captured airfield nearby and attacked the Lightnings, precipitating a brief but deadly dogfight. Before the participants finally came to their senses and backed off, two P-38 pilots had been killed, at least one Yak shot down and several other aircraft on both sides damaged. This became a serious international incident, straining US/Soviet relations and resulting in Col Edwinson being relieved of his command.

The group continued to fly tedious and mostly uneventful long-range bomber escort missions until the end of the war. Its increasingly frequent dive-bombing and strafing assignments were, on the other hand, often quite exciting. The pilots became particularly adept at 'loco-busting', running up an impressive score of destroyed locomotives. However, the numerous and extremely efficient German flak gunners made this a very dangerous 'sport'.

Lt Ken Frost peers out from the cockpit of his P-38J-15 *BATTLIN' BET* (42-104044/'BB'). Frost damaged a Bf 109 over Munich during a 'Photo Freddie' escort on 6 November 1944, exactly three months after destroying an He 111 on the ground in Rumania while returning from a Russian shuttle mission (*Thomas Van Stein*)

There was a brief rise in the number of enemy aircraft being encountered in the air during March 1945. After its usual bomber escort mission on the 21st, the group flew a fighter sweep over Hungary on the way home. Six Fw 190s were seen taking off from the Papa airfield, and one of them was shot down by a 96th FS pilot. The following day's mission was almost identical, and once again enemy aircraft were spotted over Papa and another Fw 190 and a Bf 109 were downed, this time by the 97th FS. Other pilots from the squadron strafed a nearby landing ground and destroyed ten more enemy aircraft – Lt James M 'Mel' Dolan was credited with five of them, for which he was awarded a Silver Star.

Other combat veterans joined (or rejoined) the 82nd FG for their second tours around this time. Capt Herman Visscher arrived on 15 March and soon became operations officer of his old 97th FS. Also assigned to the group that day was Maj Verl E Jett, a seven-victory ace who had served with the 8th and 475th FGs in New Guinea, flying both P-39s and P-38s. He was made operations officer of the 96th FS. In April Capt John Litchfield and 1Lt Harlon Conger returned for their second combat tours. Litchfield had been the 97th's CO a year earlier, but this time he was assigned to the 96th. 'Jake' Conger, who had been kicked out of the group for insubordination during his first tour, rejoined the 95th FS. Assigned to the 97th that month was Maj Warren R Lewis, who, like Maj Jett, had scored seven confirmed kills whilst serving in New Guinea with the 475th FG.

On the last day of March the 31st FG finally 'dethroned' the 82nd as the top-scoring USAAF fighter group in the MTO – a distinction it had held for more than two years. The group's last aircraft claim was on 8 April, when a Bf 109 was damaged over Linz, in Austria. This brought the 82nd's total to 548 aircraft destroyed, 90 probably destroyed and 227 damaged in the air, plus 176 destroyed on the ground. Its pilots included 26 bona fide aces, and a few others who came very close to achieving that distinction.

APPENDICES

Aces and near-Aces of the 82nd FG (pilots with four or more confirmed aerial victories)

Name (and Squadron)	Official Aerial Credits	Ground Claims and Comments
William J Sloan (96th)	12/0/5	
Louis E Curdes (95th)	9/0/2	PoW 27/8/43 (released), includes 1/0/0 with Fifth Air Force
Frank D Hurlbut (96th)	9/1/4	
Walter J Carroll Jr (96th)	7/1/0	Killed in flying accident USA 20/1/45
Claude R Kinsey Jr (96th)	7/2/1	PoW 5/4/43 (escaped)
Verl E Jett (96th)	7/0/1	all with Fifth Air Force
Clarence O Johnson (96th)	7/3/1	includes 3/0/0 and 6/0/0 ground with Eighth Air Force, KIA Holland 23/9/44
Ward A Kuentzel (96th)	7/0/5	KIA France 19/6/44
Warren R Lewis (97th)	7/5/3	all with Fifth Air Force
Lawrence P Liebers (96th)	7/0/5	
Harley C Vaughn (96th)	7/1/0	
Edward T Waters (96th)	7/0/1	
Charles E Adams Jr (95th)	6/0/0	2/0/0 ground
James D Holloway (95th)	6/0/1	2/0/1 ground, KIA Burma 18/6/45
William J Schildt (95th)	6/2/0	0/0/0.5 ground
Thomas A White (97th)	6/1/0	Wounded 25/3/43
Charles J Zubarik (96th)	6/0/1	PoW 24/5/43
Leslie E Andersen (96th)	5/1/0	
Paul R Cochran (96th)	5/0/0	includes 1/0/0 with 14th FG
Claud E Ford (95th and 97th)	5/1/1.5	5/0/2 ground
Warner F Gardner (95th)	5/0/2	0/0/1 ground
Robert C Griffith (97th)	5/1/2	7/0/0 ground, KIA 26/7/44
T H McArthur (95th)	5/1/0	Killed in flying accident 3/5/43
Ernest K Osher (95th)	5/0/2	
Gerald L Rounds (97th)	5/1/2	
Herman W Visscher (97th)	5/2/0	+1/0/0 in Korean War
Merrill M Adelson (96th)	4/2/0	2/0/0 ground
Lloyd E Atteberry (97th)	4/0/1	KIA 22/3/43
Joseph F Belton Jr (95th)	4/0/0	2/0/0 ground
Richard M Gangel (96th)	4/0/0	2/0/1 ground
James R Gant (95th)	4/0/0	
Alex K Hamric (95th)	4/0/1	KIA 11/4/43
Clayton M Isaacson (96th)	4/1/1.5	1/1/1 ground
Jack D Joley (95th)	4/0/0	4/0/0 ground
Joseph W Jorda (96th)	4/2/1	
Richard F Kenney Jr (95th)	4/0/1	PoW 15/6/43
Arthur W Kidder Jr (96th)	4/0/1	1/0/0 ground
Robert E Kirtley (95th)	4/2/2	includes 0/1/1 with 1st FG
Roland O Leeman (95th)	4/0/4	3/0.5/0 ground
LeRoy L Lette (97th)	4/0/1	3/0/0 ground
Paul R Mass (95th)	4/0/0	2/0/0 ground
Sammy E McGuffin (97th)	4/1/2	1/0/0 ground
Marion Moore (95th)	4/0/0	
Robert W Muir (95th)	4/1/0	
John A Perrone (96th)	4/0/0	
William B Rawson (96th)	4/1/3	KIA 11/4/43
Philip D Rodgers (96th)	4/0/3	
Daniel F Sharp (95th)	4/3/1	
Jack G Walker (97th)	4/3/1	
Fred J Wolfe (96th)	4/0/0	

1

P-38E 41-2092 of SSgt William J Schildt, 95th FS, Mines Field, Los Angeles, California, June 1942

Future ace Bill Schildt flew this aircraft until it was transferred later that summer to the 54th FS in Alaska, where it participated in the Aleutians campaign. The veteran fighter was eventually destroyed in a crash there on 29 December 1944, killing its pilot, Lt James Reys.

2

P-38E 41-2223 of Capt Robert E Kirtley, 95th FS, Mines Field, Los Angeles, California, June 1942

Bob Kirtley assumed command of the 95th PS effective 1 May 1942 after transferring from the 1st PG. This Lightning was destroyed in a taxiing accident at March Field, California, on 19 July 1942 with SSgt Jim Obermiller at its controls. Kirtley's subsequent combat tour in North Africa with both the 82nd and 1st FGs resulted in a score of four enemy aircraft destroyed, two probables and two damaged.

3

P-38G-1 42-12727 of Capt Harley C Vaughn, 96th FS, Glendale, California, July 1942

Another 1st PG transferee, Vaughn became CO of the 96th FS on 13 July 1942. His P-38 was one of only a handful of G-models received by the group before it went overseas. The 96th, unlike the 95th FS, did not paint individual aircraft numbers on its aeroplanes.

4

P-38F-15 43-2064 of 2Lt William J Sloan, 96th FS, Telergma, Algeria, February 1943

Former sergeant pilot 'Dixie' Sloan was evidently assigned this P-38 shortly after scoring his third and fourth victories on 2 February 1943, the aircraft he was flying that day having been severely damaged by an Fw 190. It is depicted here prior to the future ace having the name *Snooks* (Sloan's nickname for his wife) painted onto its nose. Lt Sloan claimed his fifth kill on 15 February – probably in this aircraft – to become the group's first ace.

5

P-38G-10 42-12871 *Milly* of 1Lt Claude R Kinsey Jr, 96th FS, Berteaux, Algeria, April 1943

Whilst in Northern Ireland, 'Kelly' Kinsey, another of the group's original staff sergeant pilots, was assigned P-38G-1 42-12787 (which he also named *Milly* after his girlfriend back in California), but he had to give it up to the 1st FG after arriving in North Africa. Kinsey was subsequently issued with 42-12871, which had been transferred to the 82nd FG from the 78th FG in England in February 1943. Kinsey was the top-scoring P-38 pilot in the MTO when he was shot down (most likely in this aeroplane) and taken prisoner on 5 April. He had downed two Ju 52/3ms that day to bring his score to seven destroyed, two probables and one damaged. Kinsey's only documented victory in 42-12871 was the unidentified Italian fighter he shot down east of Pantellaria on 20 March.

6

P-38G-10 42-13194 *TWIN ENGIN INJUN II* of Maj Harley C Vaughn, 96th FS, Berteaux, Algeria, April 1943

Vaughn remained in command of the 96th FS until the end of June 1943, by which time he had scored seven confirmed and one probable victories. He began flying 42-13194 that spring, his first *TWIN ENGIN INJUN* having almost certainly been P-38G-5 42-12827, with which he scored his fourth kill (a Ju 88) on 20 March. 42-13194 was shot down by a Bf 109 over Italy on 20 August 1943 and its pilot, 2Lt Erwin Antilla of the 97th FS, killed.

7

P-38G-10 42-13054 *Pearl III* of 1Lt Charles J Zubarik, 96th FS, Berteaux, Algeria, May 1943

Former sergeant pilot 'Ricky' Zubarik claimed six confirmed kills before he was shot down in another P-38 and taken prisoner on 24 May 1943. He is known to have scored at least two of his victories – a pair of Bf 109s on 20 March – in *Pearl III* (which he named after his mother). The aeroplane's victory markings include two question marks, representing the Me 210s that collided while manoeuvring to attack him on 6 May and for which he received no official credit. 42-13054 met its end on 24 June 1944 when a 97th FS pilot crash-landed the fighter at Vincenzo, in Italy.

8

P-38F-15 43-2112 *"THE SAD SACK"* of Maj Ernest K Osher, 95th FS, Berteaux, Algeria, May 1943

'Hawk' Osher was another of the 1st PG pilots who transferred to the 82nd in California. He became CO of the 95th FS effective 1 May 1943 and flew his 50th, and last, mission on 21 June, although he remained in command of the squadron until 26 July. He was at the controls of 'AS', which had a reputation for being a particularly reliable and well-performing aircraft, on 31 of his 50 combat missions. The fighter had also been flown by his predecessor, Maj Kirtley, who destroyed a Ju 88 and an Ar 196 in it on 21 February. Osher claimed his third and fourth kills (a C.200 and an SM.82) with *"THE SAD SACK"* on 5 May and became an ace when they shot down a Bf 109 together on 11 May. By that time 'AS' had scored 11 confirmed victories. Among the other 95th FS pilots to see combat in 43-2112 was Lt John Cappo, who made all his aerial claims in it – two Ju 52/3ms destroyed on 11 April and a Bf 109 destroyed and another probably destroyed on 29 April. Also, 96th FS ace 'Dixie' Sloan had scored his first kill, and the group's first over North Africa, in 43-2112 on 7 January.

9

P-38G-5 42-12832 of 2Lt Louis E Curdes, 95th FS, Souk-el-Arba, Algeria, June 1943

Lou Curdes joined the 95th FS in mid-April 1943, and on the 29th of that month shot down three Bf 109s and damaged another. He became an ace on 19 May when he downed two more Bf 109s, most likely in this aircraft. He destroyed a C.202 on 24 June and damaged another Bf 109 on 30 July.

When Curdes was shot down over Italy on 27 August he was flying P-38G-10 42-13150, coded 'AZ'. He was released from an Italian prison in September but wandered behind the lines for eight months before meeting up with Allied soldiers. Curdes then claimed and was awarded official credit for the two Bf 109s he had shot down on his last mission, bringing his total to eight destroyed and two damaged. In the meantime, 42-12832 had been lost to flak over Italy on 4 September whilst being flown by 2Lt John Winney, who was killed. Despite his ordeal, Curdes volunteered for another combat tour and ended up in the Philippines flying P-51s with the 3rd Air Commando Group, with which he shot down a Japanese reconnaissance aircraft.

10

P-38G-15 43-2406 CAT SASS of 1Lt William J Schildt, 95th FS, Souk-el-Arba, Algeria, July 1943

Schildt was assigned P-38F-15 43-2069 in Ireland and flew it to Algeria on 23 December 1942. He continued to use the aircraft, and 14 other Lightnings, over the next three months. Amongst the latter machines were P-38G-5 42-12806, with which he scored a probable Bf 109 on 29 January and destroyed a Bf 110 on 31 January, P-38F-5 42-12612, in which he claimed another probable Bf 109 on 28 February, and P-38F-15 43-2082, with which he shot down a Bf 109 on 10 April and three Ju 52/3ms the following day, making him an ace. Schildt was sent to rest camp after crashing 43-2082 at Bône at the completion of the latter mission. When he returned he was assigned 43-2406, which he flew on most of his remaining missions, and with which he scored his sixth victory, an Italian seaplane, on 14 May. Schildt's 50th, and last, combat mission was on 17 July. 43-2406 was destroyed in a landing accident at Foggia, in Italy, on 11 January 1944.

11

P-38G-5 42-12835 Snooks IV½ of 1Lt William J Sloan, 96th FS, Souk-el-Arba, Algeria, July 1943

This was 'Dixie' Sloan's last assigned P-38, which was also named after his wife and with which he scored most, if not all, of his later victories, the last of which was a Bf 109 on 22 July 1943 that raised his score to 12 destroyed and five damaged. When he went home in early August he was not only the group's highest-scoring pilot, but the top USAAF ace in the MTO at that time. Later in the year 'BO' was assigned to Lt Charles Pinson, who named it Penny after his sister.

12

P-38G (serial unknown) CADIZ EAGLE of 1Lt Gerald L Rounds, 97th FS, Souk-el-Arba, Algeria, July 1943

This was the Lightning former sergeant pilot Gerry Rounds flew during the late spring and summer of 1943. He scored his fourth kill, a Bf 109, with it on 5 July.

13

P-38G-10 42-13174 Hell's Angel of Flt Off Frank J Hurlbut, 96th FS, Souk-el-Arba, Algeria, August 1943

Hurlbut flew this Lightning during the latter part of his tour, including the 2 September 1943 DUC mission to Naples that saw him claim his ninth, and last, victory. The fighter's name appeared on the right side of the nose only, and sadly there is no photograph available showing this marking.

14

P-38F-15 43-2181 My Baby of 1Lt Wilbur S Hattendorf, 95th FS, Grombalia, Tunisia, August 1943

After its arrival in England in November 1942, 43-2181 was assigned to the 78th FG, one of whose pilots flew it to Casablanca in February. The fighter was then flown to the 82nd FG at Telergma, where it was assigned to veteran 95th FS pilot 'Will' Hattendorf. He named it My Baby after his wife, a painting of whom appeared on the right side of its nose. 43-2181's first air action was on 22 March 1943, when Hattendorf probably destroyed a Bf 109. On 5 April he used the fighter to destroy another Bf 109. Six days later Hattendorf and My Baby shot down a Ju 88 and a Bf 110. Lt Jim Gant scored the first of his four victories when he downed an Italian fighter in 43-2181 on 28 April. By the time Lt Hattendorf completed his tour on 9 August, My Baby had scored five confirmed victories and flown 60 combat missions, 38 of them with him at its controls. On 26 September four-victory 96th FS pilot (and future ace) Lt C O 'Tuffy' Johnson flew 43-2181 across the Atlantic to the USA for a War Bond tour.

15

P-38G (serial unknown) Chicken Dit of 1Lt Gerald L Rounds, 97th FS, Maddelina (Gerbini Satellite Field No 2), Sicily, September 1943

Sometime after early July Rounds changed the name of his aeroplane from CADIZ EAGLE to Chicken Dit. On 11 September he and 'CD' shot down a Bf 109 while providing cover for the Salerno landings – his fifth victory. Unfortunately, Chicken Dit was shot up in that fight and lost its hydraulics. This forced Rounds to belly-land the fighter at their temporary Sicilian base, bringing its career to an end. He completed his combat tour later that same month, having flown a total of 82 missions – an 82nd FG record.

16

P-38H-5 42-66825 Thoughts of Midnite of Capt Verl E Jett, 431st FS/475th FG, Dobodura, New Guinea, October 1943

Jett served initially with the 36th FS of the 8th FG, with which he scored one kill in a P-39 over New Guinea before transferring to the new 475th FG in July 1943. He had scored three more in P-38s with the 431st FS by the time he was appointed squadron commander in November. When he became CO he changed the number of his aeroplane from '120' to '110' and its risque name (and painting) to The Woffledigit. The name Hettie was painted on the right outboard engine cowling, and on the right side of the gun bay was a rendition of 'Fifinella', the Women's Airforce Service Pilots mascot. By the time he completed his tour in April 1944 Maj Jett had raised his score to seven destroyed and one damaged. After joining the 82nd FG's 96th FS in March 1945 he flew enough missions to earn another Air Medal.

17

P-38G-15 43-2428 TENNESSEE TODDY of Maj Hugh M Muse Jr, 95th FS, Lecce, Italy, December 1943

43-2428/'AM' was assigned initially to Lt Edward Braddock, who completed his tour with the 95th FS in July 1943 with three confirmed kills. Maj Muse, who renamed the fighter after his home state, became the squadron's new CO on the 26th of that month, just two weeks after joining it, succeeding Maj Osher. He scored one aerial victory plus three damaged, and claimed one enemy aircraft destroyed and four damaged on the ground. Muse and *TENNESSEE TODDY* were lost during the group's disastrous air battle over northern Italy on Christmas Day 1943.

18

P-38G (serial unknown) *Betty May* of 1Lt Paul F Jorgensen, 97th FS, Vincenzo (Foggia No 11), Italy, January 1944

'Jorgie' Jorgensen named this P-38 after his wife. He is known to have scored at least his third, and last, kill (a Bf 109 on 14 January) in *Betty May*, which was badly shot up in that fight. During his 50-mission tour, from August 1943 to March 1944, Lt Jorgensen also damaged two Bf 109s.

19

P-38J (serial unknown) *Janet* of Capt Thomas A White, 338th FS/55th FG, Nuthampstead, England, February 1944

'Ace' White's North African combat tour came to a premature end after only 22 missions when he was injured in a crash-landing on 25 March 1943, by which time he had already scored six confirmed kills and a probable. After recovering from his injuries he joined the 55th FG in England in December 1943 but made no further claims for enemy aircraft. The first fighter assigned to him in the 338th FS was P-38H-5 42-67030/'CL-Y', which was also named *Janet*. This Lightning replaced it. Janet was the name of the daughter of his good friend and 97th FS intelligence officer, Capt Wallace 'Uncle Wally' Reyerson. After the war White became a well-known Alaskan 'bush' pilot.

20

P-38G-15 43-2434 *Margie* of 2Lt Paul R Mass, 95th FS, Vincenzo, Italy, April 1944

Mass' first combat mission, on 12 April 1944, was in 43-2434, and the following day he shot down a Ju 88 whilst flying it over Hungary. He flew her regularly until 17 May, on which date he destroyed another Ju 88 on the ground. Unfortunately, *Margie* was damaged by flak during this mission and Lt Mass had to belly-land it at a 'friendly field', bringing the fighter's career to an end. He was then assigned his second 'A-12', P-38J-15 43-28754, with which he shot down a Bf 109 and an Me 410 on 26 June and an He 111 (and destroyed another on the ground) on 22 July. Mass flew his 52nd, and last, mission on 26 July, his final score being four destroyed in the air and two on the ground. 43-28754 was subsequently lost to flak over Yugoslavia on 21 September, its pilot, Lt Donald Swan, managing to evade capture.

21

P-38G-15 43-2489 *BARBARA ANN* of 2Lt Melvin E Wiedbusch, 95th FS, Vincenzo, Italy, April 1944

'A6', which had originally been flown by Lt Harold Farrell in North Africa, was assigned to Wiedbusch shortly after he joined the group in February 1944. He almost certainly scored all of his victories in this aeroplane – a Bf 109 on 26 March, an Fw 190 on 12 April, another Bf 109 on 13 April and a Bf 109 damaged on 23 April. Lt Wiedbusch then received brand new

P-38J-15, 43-28774, in which he was killed during a fight with Bf 109s over southern France on 25 June.

22

P-38F-15 43-2112 *"THE SAD SACK"* of 2Lt Roland O Leeman, 95th FS, Vincenzo, Italy, May 1944

By February 1944 the venerable 43-2112 had been assigned to Flt Off 'Tuffy' Leeman, its appearance having changed considerably since its North African days. The aircraft is depicted here sporting the USAAF's new blue and white star and bar insignia on its booms and wings. Its scoreboard had also been modified with the replacement of the old fasces victory symbols (signifying Italian aircraft it had shot down) with swastikas in deference to America's new ally. The meaning of the new letters 'L R P' under the nose art remains unknown. Leeman, who had joined the squadron in December, was a skilful and aggressive fighter pilot. He and 43-2112 proved to be a good match, for they destroyed an Me 210 on 24 February, damaged a Bf 109 on 30 March, shot down another Bf 109 on 3 April (shortly after Leeman had been promoted to second lieutenant), destroyed a Ju 88 on 13 April and damaged a Bf 109 on 5 May. On 28 May they destroyed three enemy aircraft on the ground. During a similar airfield strafing mission to Yugoslavia the following day, *"THE SAD SACK"* was badly shot up by flak. Leeman had to belly-land it back at Foggia and the fighter was subsequently scrapped. This amazing aircraft had flown 183 combat missions in nearly 18 months and had shot down 16 enemy aeroplanes, destroyed at least three on the ground and probably destroyed or damaged many more. Lt Leeman finished his tour the following month with a score of four destroyed and four damaged in the air and three destroyed and one shared probable on the ground.

23

P-38J-15 42-104035 of Maj Warren R Lewis, 433rd FS/ 475th FG, Biak Island, New Guinea, June 1944

As squadron commander, Maj Lewis was assigned this, the 433rd FS's first natural metal finish P-38, in early 1944. Lewis had joined the 475th FG's 431st FS in July 1943, but in November he transferred to the 433rd as its CO, in which position he served until August 1944. His final score was seven destroyed, five probables and three damaged. Lewis joined the 82nd FG's 97th FS in April 1945.

24

P-38J-15 43-28778 *Billy Boy* of Lt Col Ben A Mason, 82nd FG HQ, Vincenzo, Italy, June 1944

Mason was assigned this Lightning shortly after joining the 82nd FG as its new deputy CO in early April 1944, and he named it after his son. As to 43-28778's code letters, 'H' stood for Headquarters and 'B' identified the group's second-in-command. Lt Col Mason usually flew with the 97th, *Billy Boy* being maintained by that squadron, and he scored both of his aerial victories with it. The first was a Bf 109 on 10 May and the second a Bf 110 he claimed during the Ploesti dive-bombing mission on 10 June. Mason also destroyed five enemy aircraft on the ground. He was acting group commander from 4 August, when Lt Col Litton was posted missing in action, until 28 August, when Col Clarence Edwinson became the 82nd's new CO. 43-28778 was badly damaged in a crash-landing shortly before Mason went home in October, so he received a new *Billy Boy* (P-38L-1 44-23849), which was lost to flak over northern Italy on 22 April 1945.

25

P-38J-15 43-28679 *Sweet Sue* of 1Lt Robert C Griffith, 97th FS, Vincenzo, Italy, July 1944
Bob Griffith was assigned to the 97th FS in March 1944. On 29 May he participated in an airfield strafing mission to Yugoslavia, during which he destroyed an He 111 on the ground in a P-38G coded 'C4' (his first aerial victory had been an He 111 destroyed on 16 April). Shortly thereafter he was assigned this P-38J, which he named after his mother. Griffith was killed in action in *Sweet Sue* on 26 July whilst en route home from Russia on his 63rd mission, the victim of Rumanian Air Force Bf 109s. His final score in the air was five destroyed, one probable and two damaged, and he claimed to have destroyed seven other enemy aircraft on the ground, the latter an 82nd FG record.

26

P-38J-15 42-104179 *PENNY II* of Capt Charles H Pinson, 96th FS, Vincenzo, Italy, July 1944
Charlie Pinson joined the 96th FS in October 1943 and was initially assigned 'Dixie' Sloan's old P-38G, before receiving this J-model, which he also named after his sister. He scored his first kill, a Bf 109, on 2 April 1944, and downed another on 24 June. He led the massacre of the Luftwaffe *Zerstören* near Vienna on 8 July, during which he shot down an Me 410. Pinson (in *Penny II*) fell victim to Rumanian Bf 109s on 26 July and became a PoW, but he was released at the end of August. His final score was three destroyed and one probable in the air and one destroyed on the ground.

27

P-38J (serial unknown) *Little Claire* of 1Lt LeRoy L Lette, 97th FS, Vincenzo, Italy, July 1944
Lee Lette joined the 97th FS in March 1944 with his friend and fellow 20-year-old Bob Griffith. At first he flew an old G-model Lightning coded 'CW', but he was soon assigned this P-38J, which he named after his infant daughter. Lette flew his 51st, and last, mission on 26 July, by which time he had scored four destroyed and one damaged in the air and three destroyed on the ground.

28

P-38J-15 43-28796 *Judy Ann* of 1Lt Charles E Adams Jr, 95th FS, Vincenzo, Italy, July 1944
'Bones' Adams undertook his first mission on 25 February 1944. His first assigned fighter (also coded 'AI') was P-38G-10 42-13199, which he flew on missions from 29 March to 16 April. He scored his first victory – an Me 210 – in it on 13 April. From then until 23 June Adams flew nine other Lightnings, including P-38J-15 43-28654, with which he scored an Fw 190 on 16 June (and which was destroyed in a crash on 10 August that killed its pilot, Lt Lawrence Kinard Jr). He was then assigned 43-28796, which he named after his daughter and in which he shot down a Bf 110 on 26 June. When Adams claimed three Me 410s near Vienna on 8 July he was flying P-38J-15 44-23188 (which was lost with

Lt Elbert Creech when it crashed into the Adriatic Sea on 17 August). Adams' 50th, and last, mission was on 2 August. Besides his six aerial victories, he destroyed another two aircraft on the ground.

29

P-38J-15 42-104145 *LUCKY LADY* of Lt Col William P Litton, 82nd FG HQ, Vincenzo, Italy, August 1944
Bill Litton had seen action as a P-39 squadron CO with the 54th FG in the Aleutians in 1942. He was assigned to 82nd FG HQ as deputy group commander in September 1943 and succeeded Lt Col MacNicol as group CO after the latter's death on 21 December. By the time he was shot down in this Lightning (whose code letters identified the group commander's aircraft) on the 4 August 1944 Russian shuttle mission, Litton had been credited with destroying two enemy aircraft in the air and had claimed two more (and three damaged) on the ground. Although badly injured, he survived as a PoW and was evacuated from Rumania at the end of August. Litton usually flew with the 96th FS, and both of his aerial victories were scored with this unit. He was killed during the Korean War on 1 November 1951 while commanding the F-80-equipped 51st FW.

30

P-38J-15 43-28769 *Peg O' My Heart* of 1Lt Nathanial A Pape, 95th FS, Vincenzo, Italy, August 1944
'Nate' Pape, who joined the 95th FS in April 1944, was not an ace, but he could possibly have been one had he enjoyed better luck, or been a better shot! He claimed six Bf 109s in the air – a probable and a damaged on 5 May, two more damaged on 24 and 25 June and a confirmed and a damaged on 4 August (whilst covering 96th FS pilots Dick Willsie and Dick Andrews during the latter's famous rescue of the former in Rumania). The return trip from the Ukraine two days later was Pape's 50th, and last, mission. 43-28769 was lost with 2Lt Jerold Cookson when he crashed in northern Italy due to engine failure and bad weather on 12 January 1945.

31

P-38J-15 42-104174 *SNAKE EYES* of Capt Richard E Willsie, 96th FS, Vincenzo, Italy, August 1944
Dick Willsie transferred from the 414th NFS to the 82nd FG in December 1943. Serving for a time as 96th FS operations officer, he became squadron CO at the end of August 1944, replacing Maj Isaacson. Then-Maj Willsie completed his tour in December with 82 missions (not counting those he flew with the 414th NFS) to his name, tying 97th FS ace Gerry Rounds for the group's highest individual total. His official victory tally was two destroyed and one damaged in the air and one destroyed and one damaged on the ground, but he also lost a sure aerial kill to a coin toss. After Willsie left the squadron 42-104174 was assigned to Lt Richard Ostronik.

32

P-38J-15 42-104044 *BATTLIN BET* of 1Lt Kenneth R Frost Jr, 96th FS, Vincenzo, Italy, November 1944
Nineteen-year-old Flt Off Ken Frost joined the 96th FS on 27 June 1944 and flew his first combat mission the following day. On 7 July, after his sixth, he was assigned this aircraft. An accomplished artist, Frost painted a caricature of his

girlfriend, Betty, on its nose and named it *BATTLIN BET* (BB!) in her honour. He turned 20 later that month and was soon promoted to second lieutenant. Although not an ace, Frost was an aggressive pilot who made good use of his few opportunities in combat. He destroyed an He 111 on the ground on 6 August and damaged a Bf 109 during a 'Photo Freddie' escort on 6 November. By the time he flew his 50th, and last, mission on 17 November, Frost had also destroyed four locomotives. Four days later, 42-104044 was written off in a crash-landing by a 95th FS pilot. Lt Frost became an instructor pilot back in the US and was killed in a crash in the California desert on 17 September 1945 whilst flying P-38L-1 44-24492.

33

P-38L-5 44-25638 *ALMOST 'A' DRAGGIN* **of Maj Clayton M Isaacson, 7th FS/49th FG, Lingayen, the Philippines, May 1945**

'Ike' Isaacson joined the 82nd FG in September 1943, immediately after completing a 50-mission B-25 tour with the 321st BG. He racked up 78 more missions in P-38s and an official score of four destroyed, one probable and 1.5 damaged in the air and one destroyed, one probable and

one damaged on the ground – and commanded the 96th FS from March to August 1944. This evidently had not been enough for him, however, as Isaacson then volunteered for yet another combat tour. In February 1945 he joined the 49th FG in the Philippines as operations officer of its 7th FS. He commanded the squadron from May to July, by which time he had flown another 82 missions. Isaacson was initially assigned this aircraft, and after 'cracking it up' he received another P-38L-5, *ALMOST 'A' DRAGGIN II* (No 1), whose serial number is not known. Isaacson also flew 123 F-80 missions in Korea with the 51st FW. He retired from the USAF as a brigadier general.

34

P-38J-25 (serial unknown) of 1Lt Lawrence P Liebers, 429th FS/474th FG, Langensalza, Germany, June 1945

Larry Liebers joined the 474th FG in May 1945, shortly after VE Day – too late to see any action in the ETO. During his earlier tour with the 96th FS in North Africa, from April through to August 1943, he was credited with seven confirmed kills and five damaged. Liebers stayed in the USAAF after the war and was killed in a flying accident on 21 August 1946.

INDEX